ROUGH CROSSING

River Teeth Literary Nonfiction Prize
Daniel Lehman and Joe Mackall, SERIES EDITORS

The River Teeth Literary Nonfiction Prize is awarded to the best work of literary nonfiction submitted to the annual contest sponsored by *River Teeth: A Journal of Nonfiction Narrative*.

Also available in the River Teeth Literary Nonfiction Prize series:
The Girls in My Town: Essays by Angela Morales

ROUGH CROSSING

An Alaskan
Fisherwoman's
Memoir

Rosemary McGuire

UNIVERSITY OF NEW MEXICO PRESS | ALBUQUERQUE

Library of Congress Cataloging-in-Publication Data
Names: McGuire, Rosemary Desideria, author.
Title: Rough crossing : an Alaskan fisherwoman's memoir / Rosemary McGuire.
Other titles: Alaskan fisherwoman's memoir
Description: First edition. | Albuquerque : University of New Mexico Press, [2016] |
Series: River Teeth Literary Nonfiction Prize
Identifiers: LCCN 2016028185 (print) | LCCN 2016029028 (ebook) |
ISBN 9780826358028 (pbk. : alk. paper) | ISBN 9780826358035 (electronic)
Subjects: LCSH: McGuire, Rosemary Desideria. | Fishers—Alaska—
Biography. |Women fishers—Alaska—Biography. | Fisheries—Alaska—
Anecdotes. | Women—Alaska—Biography. | Alaska—Social life and customs.
Classification: LCC SH20.M42 A3 2016 (print) | LCC SH20.M42 (ebook) |
DDC 639.2092 [B] —dc23
LC record available at https://lccn.loc.gov/2016028185

Cover photo: *Rough Waters in Prince William Sound, December 2012*, by David P. Janka
Designed by Catherine Leonardo
Composed in Bembo Std Reg. 10.5/14
Display font is Clarendon LT Std

ROUGH CROSSING

ONE

⟿

"**KNOW ANYONE WHO** needs a deckhand?" I asked the man gutting halibut, the snow at his feet stained red with blood.

"The *Totem* might need somebody. I heard they were looking." He pointed to a power scow tied up farther down the float. Eighty feet long, the wheelhouse on the stern.

I walked up to it and called, "Hello?"

Snow covered the deck, scuffed with footsteps, but the cabin lights were off. I climbed on deck and knocked at the door. There was no answer.

Another man trudged down the dock.

"Know anyone looking for crew?" I asked.

But the man passing shook his head. Two kids emerged from one of the boats, carrying trash, and disappeared as quickly as they'd come. Already dusk was falling, early yet. Voices echoed over the water from the bar. One by one, the lights of town came on. A diesel engine started. Coughed. Lines slapped against the dock. In the dim light, a boat backed, turned, and headed for the harbor entrance. Its wake veed, sending ripples that broke along the pilings of the fish dock and set the fleet bobbing slowly at its moorings. Up. Down. Up. Down. The boats rose and fell as if the surface of the water breathed beneath them, their lines hanging loose and heavy in wet weather.

On the pilings, gulls were outlined against a sleeping sky. Smell of seaweed, oil, and snow.

Two drunk men moved toward the boats.

"I told him, I said . . ." the voice of one rose briefly, futile against the day, subsiding, "he's gone." He stopped, bent to tie his shoe, and stood as if he had forgotten how to move on.

A truck passed, spraying slush from the rutted street. At this hour, the houses seemed to draw together, presenting a single darkened front to the outer world, their roofs dim triangles, black where the night's snow had sluffed away.

A sign flashed on in the window of a café. Open . . . Open . . . It flickered and died until someone, reaching, shook it violently from within.

As I walked back up the ramp, my boots scuffed snow into the water. It broke the surface into lines that spread until they lapped against the floats.

A woman came up behind me.

"Know anyone who needs a deckhand?" I stopped her as she passed.

"The *Alice* might need somebody. I heard they were looking." She pointed to another scow tied up against the transient float. I went over and shouted hello. There was no answer. Disappointed, I climbed the breakwater again. The sky had cleared with the last light, and a wind had sprung up. The boats rocked and sighed at their lines. I thought they looked eager to go to sea. Like me.

I sat down. I was thinking of Nate, a clearer and less painful thought than that of the present moment. I'd known him in Fairbanks, at a bar I worked at when I lived there. He'd told me stories about fishing when I first met him, and I'd liked it, though he was older than me and skinny inside his worn-out flannel shirt. When I left town, he drove me to the station. It had snowed that night. He arrived too early, in case the roads were bad, he said. When we reached the station, he parked outside it and turned to look at me. "I've been wondering. You ever think you might come back to Fairbanks?" he asked. There was more in his words than just that. He wanted me to stay with him.

I sat picking at the fabric of my jeans. Finally, I looked at him and shook my head. I had places to go. I did not want to settle just for a man.

"Forget it," he said. "Sorry to embarrass you." He opened the truck door and swung my pack out of the back. The silence between us lasted until I said good-bye. Now he was gone. I would not see him again. And my loneliness crystallized around the fact of his absence, though I hardly knew him.

I tossed another rock into the water. It broke the surface into darkened ripples that spread until they lapped against my feet and sent reflections running out to sea. I stood up, stiff and weary, to walk the docks again.

The next morning someone had pinned a note on the bulletin board outside the harbor master's. "Deckhand needed for Togiak herring and Bristol Bay salmon seasons. Apply at the F/V *Webb-slinger*" A hand-drawn map gave directions to the boatyard.

It was a long walk from the harbor. When I found the yard, I trudged past the ranks of tarped-over yachts and fishing boats, shapeless in their coverings, waiting for spring. The *Webbslinger* lay on blocks at the end of a row. On deck, a man was grinding steel.

"Hello?" I called.

He peered over the side.

"I hear you need crew," I said.

He looked me up and down, smiled, and shook his head. "Sorry. I won't hire a girl." As if to explain, he added, "You'd be worthless on deck."

I didn't answer. I didn't trust myself to speak, but all the same, as I walked away, tears stung my eyes. I headed back out of the Homer Spit, shoes and hair soaked with rain from the sea, my pack heavy on my back—no money but tips in change from the bar job up in Fairbanks. I'd come to Homer looking for a fresh start, for adventure and escape. I didn't know yet that running away to sea is always as much about what you run from, a life that seems to have lost its color, as it is about what you run to. That the magic of it will always brighten in daydreams, somewhere just past the next horizon. Though I'd come looking for a wilderness, now that I was here, at the bitter edge of land, I wasn't sure what to do next.

As I passed the bar I heard a shout. Two men came out and followed me down the street.

"You the girl that's looking for work?"

"I am," I said. "You looking for crew?"

"Yeah," one said. He was drunk. "I'm gonna fire mine. Coupla lazy sonsabitches. Coupla motherfuckers. I can't even find them. If I could find them, I'd fire them right now." He spat tobacco in the snow. "Are you sure you can work? I've never hired a girl, but Jesus, I gotta go fishing. Show me your hands . . . "

I held them out hopefully, small, slim-fingered hands pink with cold.

"Oh for fuck sake, you don't even have calluses. Why in hell would a girl like you want to go fishing?"

I tried to speak, but he wasn't listening. The other man slapped me on the back. He was huge, his hands raddled with work.

"This the girl gonna work with us, Boss?"

"Look at her, Everett. Just look. She's not even a large girl. If I hire her, you're going to have to pick up slack. It ain't going to be like having Troy and Troy around to help out."

"Troy and Troy are a coupla sonsabitches," Everett said. "Hell, I can do twice as much as them alone."

"Think she can do it, Everett?" the skipper asked. "It's your call. You'll pick up the slack if she doesn't."

4

"She can do it, Boss. Look in her eyes. She's got it," Everett said. He swayed as he spoke, dizzy with alcohol, and I knew he wasn't truly seeing me.

"You want the job?" the skipper asked. "When we're out there, you know, we ain't coming back. I don't want you puking up and whining to come back to land again. You gonna get seasick on me?"

"I don't know," I said, but they didn't hear me. Somehow, I felt diminished, almost child sized, talking to them.

"Look in her eyes, Boss. She's got it," Everett said again. "You want a drink, girl? Hey, you hungry? Come down to the boat, and I'll fix you something."

"Yeah, have a look at the boat." The other man spat. "Jesus, I don't know what I'm doing. Everett!"

"Yes, Boss?"

"This is a woman here, you're gonna be working with her. I don't want no hanky-panky. Anything goes on, you guys gotta keep it to yourselves."

"Hey, look, I'm looking for a job. That's all," I protested.

"You want the job, you got it. Gotta have somebody. Tell me you want it!"

"Tell her she wants it, Boss." Everett steered us down into the harbor. He stopped at the *Arctic Storm* and stepped aboard with a thud that shook the boat. Inside, the cabin was dark and filthy. An oil stove burned near the door, gloves and socks hanging over it to dry. Beside it, a curtain, half-fallen from its hooks, exposed a toilet.

"This here's the galley," the skipper said. "The wheelhouse is up above. That's the head. Use it. I might hire a woman, but I won't have her pissing over the side."

"What do you fish for?" I fumbled for a question.

"Gray cod. We're pot fishing, but we don't have a block so we're slower than most of the boats," he said. "We'll stay out three days at a time. That's as long as we can hold them before delivering. You

5

come with us, you can expect to make a hundred, two hundred dollars a day." He squeezed along the galley table. "You fixing food, Everett?"

"Yeah." Everett dragged a pan onto the stove, slapped slices of baloney into it. When the water boiled he dumped in a pack of instant noodles and stirred it quickly with his hand.

"I'll have some food for you in a minute, girl," he said. He slapped the meal on paper plates and dealt them out like a hand of cards. I swallowed it as quickly as I could—as if I could keep from touching it.

"There's more," he offered.

I shook my head.

"Hey, you never said if you got seasick," the skipper said. "You prone to getting seasick? Motion sickness?"

"No," I said. "I don't get sick."

He looked at me, a look as doubtful as I felt.

I stood up. "Guess I'll get my gear."

"We'll be leaving at four a.m.," the skipper said. "You'd sure as fuck better be back, cause we ain't waiting." He looked at me again and shook his head. As I walked back down the dock I heard them arguing.

"Didn't you look at her?"

"She's got the stuff."

I hunched my shoulders, not sure that he was right.

It was past midnight when I returned. The harbor was dark. Only the *Arctic Storm* still showed lights in its cabin. I knocked on the door, but there was no answer. I turned the handle and walked in. Everett lay passed out by the door, his backside hanging half out of his sweats. The skipper was slumped over the cabin table, an older woman beside him. Her long black hair hung limply down, and her face was creased and swollen with alcohol. Blue shadows ran in the wrinkles around her eyes. On the TV, a science fiction movie blared, but neither of the two looked at the screen. They stared into space alone, indifferent to each other and to me.

"Thought we'd seen the last of you. I was all set to call the owner and tell him he needed to come on down cause we were short a deckhand," the skipper said without looking up.

"It was a long walk. I couldn't get a ride in the dark."

"So you gonna work? I gotta go. I gotta go home," the woman said. Her head dipped toward the table.

"Hey, you can't sleep here," the skipper shook her. Her eyes flew open.

"Get off the boat," he said.

"'S okay. I'm going home," she mumbled. But she didn't stand up.

I tried to smile at her, but she turned her face away.

"What are you looking at?" she said.

I opened my mouth to ask if she was all right. Closed it again, knowing she did not want my help, feeling sick for not helping and not knowing what to do. I pushed aside the junk that filled my bunk and crawled into it, fully clothed and not caring, too tired to think, so tired that I wasn't even afraid.

"Everett pissed himself," she said.

"Don't fucking tell her that!" the skipper said.

I pulled the sleeping bag over my face, pretending not to hear. But it was a long time before I slept.

TWO

~

I WOKE TO daylight and a blare of harbor noise. The skipper stood over me, shaking my shoulder with a heavy hand.

"Get up," he said, and shouted again, "Everett! Get going!"

Everett crawled from his bunk.

"You're still here," he said to me.

He edged his way on deck. "Gonna go get a pop. Best hangover medicine," he spoke over his shoulder.

"Ah, Christ," the skipper cursed mechanically.

He sat down and clicked a movie on. A cheerleader pulled another girl's hair in a locker room, their panties slipping. I poured a cup of coffee and stood drinking it to the sound of their squeals and shrieks.

Last chance to quit, I thought. *I could walk off right now.*

But I didn't. I needed the job. I was nearly out of money, and, more than that, I wanted to go, to see the ocean as I had imagined it. I wanted sea and wind and stories, adventure, dawns, and the raw clean smell of far-from-land. I did not want to wonder what the world was like, but to touch it, taste it, feel and see it.

An hour later we untied. I stood on deck as we left the harbor, past the breakwater and the canneries, out to the widening water.

The raw spring land fell behind us. We were left alone with the sea. I thrilled to it, as out of place as I was.

It was a windy day, and cold. At last I turned and went into the cabin. The boat rocked to a gathering swell. Videotapes and ketchup slid across the table. I gathered them up. Socks swung above the stove to the soft *click-clack-swish* of moving food cartons on the shelves, the clothesline tapping on the wall and boots tumbling at the foot of the wheelhouse ladder: a soft noise, somehow disorienting and hard to ignore, wearying in its very repetition. Clothes piled in the fo'c'sle, woolen jackets and flannel shirts. Years ago, my mother taught me how to make quilts and rugs out of such things. It was a skill already outdated years before I was born, the kind of precious, useless thing I'd grown up somehow thinking was all I needed to know.

The skipper lit a cigarette in the wheelhouse and the smoke sank down, curling against me in the galley. Suddenly, I knew I was going to be sick. I ran for the door, hung over the side, and vomited convulsively. It didn't feel like nausea so much as it felt like my body was trying to destroy itself. At last I stopped spasming, but I didn't straighten up. I lay against the rail, seawater soaking through my coat, letting my body twist with the water motion. As we rose with the crest, miles of turbulent water unfurled before us. Fear mixed with the misery in the pit of my belly. The ocean was too big for me.

A long while passed. I crept back inside, heavy with shame. I'd lied to the men. I'd known I would get sick. On road trips, I'd always been the kid throwing up in the back seat of the pickup while my older sister scolded me. But I'd thought—hoped—that I could tough it out.

The skipper called down, "Don't you go on deck without telling me first."

"Sorry," I said. I stumbled to my bunk and sat down, head in my lap. My Xtratufs tumbled at my feet, and I thought, if the worse came to the worst, I could vomit into them.

The skipper thrust his head down from the wheelhouse. "Are you sick already? Jesus. Am I gonna have to turn this boat around and leave you in Homer? Tell me right now."

"I'll be fine," I said. I wouldn't give him the satisfaction of pity.

"You'd fucking better be fine, cause I don't want to turn around." Everett handed me a fistful of saltines. "Eat," he said. "You don't want to be throwing up on an empty stomach."

His eyes were kind. Obedient, I pushed a cracker into my mouth.

"You'll be okay," Everett assured me. "I've seen lots of guys be sick. They always get over it in a day or two and then they're fine."

He squeezed in at the table across from me and tugged a pack of cards from his pocket. "Watch!" he said. "Now pick a card."

I took a card, looked at it, and handed it back, mouthing at the crumbs that coated my dry tongue. I couldn't swallow.

"I've been fishing since I was eight," Everett said. "Six brothers and sisters, and they're all fishermen, too. Bering Sea crabbers." He dealt the cards out faceup in four rows. "Tell me which row your card's in."

Numbly, I pointed. He slid the cards together.

"I used to have a restaurant in Kansas, with a wife," he went on. "When she got the divorce she took it all. So I came fishing again. I went back there one time and I seen her in a bar, with a guy. Guy says, 'You better leave her alone, I'm a cop.' I said, 'Oh yeah, well I'm a fucking fisherman,' and I broke his nose. In jail is where you learn card tricks. Show me which row your card's in."

Again I pointed. He re-dealt, grinning.

"You should be glad you're not on a crabber. Last year, there was one guy got so chickenshit he climbed up in the stack and hid for days. Guys thought he'd fallen overboard. We was all supposed to be looking for him. Finally, he snuck down to the galley and they caught him. He was lucky he didn't go overboard then. Some guys would've thought, 'Well, chickenshit, everybody thinks you're dead anyway, so over the side with you.'"

"Jesus."

He shrugged. "It happens."

Twice more, he had me point. He swept the cards up, shuffled, and dealt, turning them faceup as he slapped them out. Halfway through the pack he looked up and grinned again. "Bet you five dollars the next card I turn over is yours."

"Okay." I managed a nod. He flipped over my card. I tried to smile, but my mouth was full of bitterness. I bolted for the door once more and hung on the rail, retching.

Everett came out on deck with more saltines and a pop for me. "Gotta keep eating, girl," he said. "Boss says we're supposed to cut bait." He opened a ten-pound box of frozen herring and dumped it out in a solid mass, took a cleaver from beside the door, and hacked heavily at the block, his arm fat with fading muscle. A chunk of herring chipped off and spun across the deck. "Hey, you know how to filet fish?"

"No."

"Damn. I was hoping. Skipper has us process fish on board. I can't fucking filet fish all lah-di-dah. Fuck that shit. The fuckers come out looking like shit." He held up his hands, the fingers swollen, seamed, and enlarged from years of work in the cold. "I can't even bend my fucking fingers some days. Chilean dude I worked with told me to piss on my hands when they get like that. You know what happens when you do that? You get pissy fingers. That's it."

The skipper shouted from inside, "You guys got that bait chopped? We're coming up on a string."

Everett grabbed a pair of orange rain pants, forced his legs into them, and handed me another pair.

"You can wear Troy's," he said.

I tried, but they came far past my feet. The skipper cut the throttle and came to stand in the doorway, laughing.

"Belt that in or we'll be using you as a sail." He flipped me a length of line with a sheath knife attached. "I don't ever want to see you on deck without that knife. If you get caught in a bight and go down with the pot you want to be able to cut yourself free." He went back inside.

Everett tossed me a pair of rubber gloves, too big for my hands. "Yeah. When we're out there, don't get in a bight," he said.

"What does that mean?" I asked.

Everett stared at me, confused. "It means . . . don't get in a bight. Don't fucking do it."

"But what's a bight?"

"It's a . . . it's like a bight," he said.

"Oh," I said.

The boat idled close in against the shore. Ahead, cliffs fell steeply down below the clouds. At the water's edge, a line of buoys rose and fell in a glassy swell that curved and broke against the overhanging, hollowed smooth rock. The tide was high, and the water rose into the boughs of the overhanging spruce that clung where they could against the granite. Snow streaked their crowns. I could smell the coldness of it, and the sharp scent of spruce needles, brackish seaweed against the rocks.

"Coming up on it now!" the skipper shouted from above. Everett ran forward, grabbed a hook, and hung over the rail as the *Arctic Storm* nosed past.

Abruptly, he straightened and flung down the hook.

"What the fuck?" the skipper shouted, leaning out the wheelhouse window.

"Can't do her, Boss. She's straight up an' down!" Everett yelled back. He muttered under his breath to me, "That's the way to fucking break an arm."

"Fu-uck," the skipper groaned. "We'll go on to the next one."

"What's wrong?" I asked.

"Tide's too high. Spring tide."

I looked back. The buoy floated halfway underwater, its line pulled tight by the force of the running tide, and the water slapping against it had an ugly look.

"Too high?" I said. I didn't understand.

"No slack," he said, and shrugged. That was it. It was a while before I understood that he needed slack to get the line around the winch drum to lift the pot. The pot was too heavy to dead-lift in the water, and the lines were too short.

The next pot lay in shallower water. Everett hooked the buoy and dragged it aboard.

"Hydraulics," he shouted. He strained against the line, trying to bring it in as the boat slid past. I took hold, but he thrust me aside.

"It's getting away from me, Boss!" he yelled.

"Don't fucking stand there, girl, help him," the skipper shouted. "For fuck sake, Everett, don't just pull, get a wrap on the drum."

He swung down the ladder and grabbed the line himself, hanging on while Everett hauled it across the deck, and took three turns around the drum barrel of the deck winch as he hit the switch to start the hydraulics. The winch rolled against the line, bringing it in. Everett dragged it hand over hand, keeping the tension on while he coiled it at his feet.

A moment later Everett was gasping for air.

"You take it, girl. Don't let it slip." I took the incoming line out of his hand. But it refused to coil as it had for him. It slid back and forth across the deck.

"Don't let yourself get in a bight, girl," the skipper warned me again. "If you get a foot caught in that line and the pot goes overboard, you're going with it." I nodded, understanding at last, and kept on, struggling to stay ahead of the line. The too-large gloves hindered me now. I threw them off and coiled bare-handed with burning palms.

"Pot's coming," Everett shouted as it struck the bottom of the boat.

"What?" This time I guessed what he wanted. But I didn't react quickly enough.

"For fuck sake, quit pulling!" the skipper yelled. "Just tally on the line." I held it steady. The men grabbed hold of the pot, hanging half over the rail. "Bring it in!"

I hauled on the line. The pot rose up, level with the rail.

"STOP!" he shouted.

I held it steady again, and they heaved the pot over the side onto the deck. The boat shuddered with the impact, and the men slumped against the rail, gasping for breath, their mouths fallen slack and open as if they'd expended the last of their volition in the act. The pot leaned between them, a cage of old steel bars and reddish web. Inside, two sea stars the color of clotted blood half covered a single thrashing cod.

"Aw, Jesus. One fish," Everett moaned.

"Jesus," I echoed him in disbelief.

He reached into the pot and grabbed the cod.

"You bleed it like this." He held it up before my eyes and wrenched out its gills, releasing a flood of dark blood. Its mouth yawned open, and it went limp in death.

"Now get your arm in there and get the bait bag out. Clip a new one in." He showed me, grabbing a loose mesh bag of half-defrosted herring, snapping it top and bottom into the pot. He broke off in a laugh. "If you were on deck with one of my sisters, they'd've chewed you up by now for not knowing shit."

The skipper scrambled back up on the bridge. "Get ready," he called. Everett took hold of the pot. I did, too.

"Splash her," he shouted down.

We threw our weight against the pot. It didn't move. I didn't yet know how to use my body, nor did I have the strength to move something so heavy. Everett shoved me back with his elbow, grabbed at the center, and single-handedly heaved it overboard. Spinning, he snatched the coiled line and the buoy, sent it flying after the pot, and fell to his knees.

I stared at him. The skipper hollered out the window, "Don't fucking do dumb shit like that, Everett, you'll get yourself a fucking hernia. I need you."

"I'm okay, Boss." Everett spoke with difficulty. He did not straighten up.

"Next time I'll come down and help you. And use the girl. She's not here to admire you."

"Okay."

"We're coming up on another pot now. Get ready," he said. But again, it was half-buried in the sea, and we hauled no more pots that afternoon. Already the light was fading from the sky. After checking that buoy and the next, the skipper called it off.

"It's not worth killing ourselves over."

We dropped anchor close behind the island, where we could find a purchase for the hook. The seas were rough there, but the main thrust of the sea was broken. It rolled past outside us, water darkening into night, seeming almost a living thing to me. The cliffs were black and wet with recent rain, streaked with old snow. I stayed on deck for a long time as the waves of sickness subsided, gulping the cold air, glad to be alive. Hard as the day had been, I was happy to be there.

When I stepped inside, Everett was frying chicken. Again, he used his hands as his only utensils, but this time, watching him, I didn't mind. I was hungry. He grinned at me, and I smiled back.

"Hungry?" he asked.

"Yeah," I said. It occurred to me that I shouldn't just stand by, waiting to be asked to help, but when I offered he shook his head.

"You go lie down. I'll call you when it's ready," he said, smiling at me. Suddenly, he seemed less of a stranger. I felt a rush of gratitude, believing he was trying to be kind.

"You didn't do so badly today," the skipper said. "It's a bitch fishing without a block. The guys who have one can haul pots all day and into the night. Block just picks the pots up off the ocean bottom. Two minutes and you're on to the next one. That's the way to make money."

"Yeah?" I said. I wondered what a block was but didn't ask.

"Trouble is, the owner doesn't give a shit about this boat, whether it makes money or doesn't or sinks or what all. He bought it for his kid to fish with, kid died right after," the skipper went on. "Ain't that food ready yet, Everett?"

In the morning I woke to find that fresh snow had fallen. The skipper sent me to sweep it off the deck while Everett made coffee. I stood outside, brushing the snow away, while inside Everett was coughing hard. He spat out the door into the snow. His spit was bloody. It left a dark stain on the deck.

"You okay?" I asked, looking at the stain.

"Yeah," he said. But he looked pale. He kept coughing into his hand as we ate.

"Hope you didn't bust something yesterday, Everett. Throwing that pot overboard like that, that was a stupid thing to do," the skipper said.

Everett pretended he hadn't heard.

"Can you work? Do you want me to take you in? You've got to tell me, Everett."

"I'll be fine." Everett looked up, offended. "It ain't TB. I get tested every time I go to jail. Lungs are bad, though. I drowned once. Southeast seining. I got caught in the net and drug over. Buddy of mine saved me—gaffed me in the back. I still got the scar." He turned his back to us, pushed up his sweat shirt, and showed a long, white scar over his kidneys.

"Well, you tell me if you decide you want to go in," the skipper said.

After we ate, we headed out to sea. But the first pot we pulled was empty.

"It's those guys with blocks," Everett said. "They can haul pots so fast, they just fish everybody else's at night." I looked at him, doubtful, but didn't argue. This time, the skipper came on deck to help us launch. The pot lurched over, splashed, and Everett collapsed across the rail, struggling for breath. He tried to stand up, then went into a paroxysm of coughing that spattered the water with blood.

"Oh, fuck it, Everett, I'm taking you in to a doctor. You're going to fucking die on me," the skipper said.

"I can work," Everett said.

"We're going in," the skipper said again.

Everett said nothing, but he looked sullen. After the skipper went back inside, Everett said to me, "I can outwork any fucker around." He turned the deck hose on to sluice seaweed overboard. "One time, I was in town. Didn't want to go fishing, but this skipper I knew came up to me and said, 'Everett, my crew doesn't know shit. You've gotta help me out here.' I told him I wasn't going, and he says, 'Well come on down to the boat and we'll talk it over.' He had a bottle of whiskey with him. Next thing I know, we're out of sight of land. Man, I taught that crew how to work, all right."

"He kidnapped you?"

"It happens. Some skippers will do anything for a good deckhand. I'm a good deckhand. I don't need no doctor. I'll be out here again in the morning. You gonna stick around?"

"If you guys go out again, I'll go with you," I said. I opened my mouth to try to explain, but closed it again without saying anything. I would not quit as easily as that.

"I thought that maybe you wasn't going to go out fishing with us no more. Thought you maybe didn't like it," Everett said.

"I'll be back."

"I'll make a fucking deckhand out of you yet." Everett turned off the hose. "Man, you've got a funny voice, though. 'Squeak squeak! Squeak squeak!' just like a mouse. I'm used to hearing guys like this—" he dropped his voice to a deep rumble and rolled out a string of swear words, "'aw shit, goddamn.' And I hear you on deck going 'Squeak squeak!' Surprises me every time."

Everett crawled into his bunk when we went inside. I sat at the table with a book, now used to bracing against the swaying boat. Inside the cover I had tucked a picture of Nate. He stood on the back of a gill-netter, mending gear on a bright-blue summer-ocean day. His shirt was off. He grinned at the camera, a wide, white, and

18

reckless smile. My thumb slid across the cold, glossy surface of the photograph.

He'd given the picture to me on our first date. It was late on a winter afternoon, the light already fading and the snow taking on a tricky glow. Somehow, I liked the look of him at once. We went across town to the Pump House bar. That day, Friday, it was already crowded, but we found a space at the back and sat down side by side on the steps leading to the fire exit.

That night we talked only about little things. But when the bar closed I let him take me home. He lived off the old Nenana highway, outside of town. Snow piled deep in the yard, plastered in wind-driven drifts. I followed him up to the door. He pushed it open with his toe. It was warm inside, and dark. A cat wound around his ankles.

"Hello, Lucy," he said. "Miss me?" He hit the light switch.

The room was small and bare, with commodity food stacked in cardboard boxes under the plywood counter. A ladder led up to a loft. Nate seemed too big for the room, but he moved with a familiar care.

"Coffee black?" he asked.

"Please," I said. He made it with a strainer, cowboy style, using good beans. We sat down awkwardly at opposite ends of the gritty couch. He held his untouched coffee, looking away. I laid my open hand on the couch. He did not reach for it. I brought it to my lap again. After a moment, I tried again, running my fingers lightly down his back. This time he took my hand. We sat like that for a long time, saying nothing. I listened to him breathe, and to the blood pounding dizzily in my veins, until he reached to kiss me. That was all.

Now I outlined his face in the photograph with my fingertip. The skipper thrust his head down through the hatch.

"What are you reading?" he said.

"Nothing," I said. I closed my book.

He reached down and took it from me. When he opened it, the picture dropped out. He picked it up and looked at it closely.

"Boyfriend?" he asked.

"Not exactly." I didn't feel like explaining.

"Well, whoever he is, he's trying to kill fish." He handed it back. "I don't know how long we're going to be in town," he said. "I'll make sure Everett gets to a doctor once we get in. If they say he can't work . . . well . . . I'll have to start looking for another deckhand. Maybe I can get the owner to come down. Are you going to be willing to come out again?"

"Yeah."

"Well you won't make much money." He had decided to tell me the truth. "The pot-fishing season's almost over anyway. We'll probably just stack out our pots and bring them in. But if you stick around, I'll fix you up with a job later. I'm going tendering here pretty quick, buying fish from the fishermen and running it back to the cannery. It's good to have a girl deckhand on a tender. Brings in the business."

"Okay," I said, not believing that he meant it or that his ideas were more than his own daydreams.

That afternoon, I stood on deck as the harbor came into sight. A shaft of light tore through heavy clouds. It towered, piling light on light, until the ocean seemed to sink beneath its weight. I watched, and suddenly the light in all its glory was blotted out by wind-driven clouds. Then there were only the mountains facing me across the bay and the bay stretching out beneath them to a winter ocean.

Everett had stepped on deck. He watched in silence for a time. Then, jerking his thumb at the surrounding sea, he said, "It's God's country, ain't it? I couldn't be anywhere else."

I smiled at him, surprised by a kind of sudden recognition. He smiled back the way a baby smiles, unsure of what it is looking at. And I believed then that we were both romantics, both in love with a wild, half-imaginary ocean.

When we reached our slip, Everett left. He said he'd walk to the clinic. I went uptown to the washeteria. The land was strange underfoot, so motionless it felt queer. I'd been gone only two days, but it seemed longer than that.

When I got back to the boat, the skipper sat at the table looking glum.

"What's up?" I said.

"I just fired Everett. I saw him in the Salty Dawg. Fucker hadn't even been to a doctor yet."

"Oh."

"I called the owner to see if he would come out fishing with us, but he said no. So I got to find another crew."

"Shoot," I said. I stood for a moment, not knowing what to do.

"We won't be going out again before tomorrow. If then. I don't know how the fuck I'm supposed to get those pots back. You can't get a crew to just go bring gear in. There's no money in it for them. You hafta force 'em somehow, like keep their paycheck on the line." He stubbed out his cigarette, shook the pack to see how many were left, and lit another. "You can stay on the boat if you need a place tonight," he offered. "Sorry you didn't make any money. You worked out okay."

"Yeah. Well, I'll be around," I said. "Thanks for the work. Let me know if something changes." But I hoisted my pack. I didn't think that anything would change.

As I walked out, the skipper called, "Remember what I said about tendering. If you need a job later, let me know."

"Thanks," I said. Out on the dock, I looked around. The harbor was as quiet as it had been before. Only I had changed in the way I saw it. It had meaning for me now, and a sense of refuge. Even the land looked different. I'd been somewhere and come back more alive than I had been. I felt elated that I'd been fishing, as if I'd finally found something hard enough for me.

THREE

THE NEXT MORNING I tried the canneries for work. At Silver Lining the manager offered me a job unloading a halibut boat. I waited on the dock as it pulled in. When the hatch was opened three of us jumped down, a kid in charge of the crew, a Native man from Fort Yukon, and me. The owner of the boat stood on deck looking down.

"Ready!" someone shouted from the pier. The crane lowered a brailer bag into the hold. All three of us began pitching fish, scooping ice out of their body cavities and tossing them into the brailer. The fish were huge, too heavy for my hands. The crew leader set a fast pace. I struggled to not fall behind.

Alongside me, the man from Fort Yukon worked steadily. "Where're you from?" he asked after a while. His voice was quiet, his words coming slow and polite.

"I grew up in Haines. Alaska."

We'd moved there when I was eight, leaving a mining claim homestead up near Fairbanks and driving to the coast in my dad's old pickup truck to a town that was small and far from everything, clutched by the sea and mountains. We'd lived in a tent there until

Dad built a cabin. My folks had been back-to-the-landers then, flower children.

"Yeah?" he said. "I went to Haines once. I haven't been back, how long."

"I knew a girl from Fort Yukon," I said. "Bonnie James. I knew her in Fairbanks."

"That so," he said.

Then there was silence for a long time as we worked. The mound of fish before us diminished slowly.

A few rockfish were mixed in with the halibut, their sides glowing the color of sunrise through the ice. We tossed those into a separate brailer bag. I began to feel curiously at home in the work, slipping into a rhythm as easy as breathing.

Growing up, I never worked on boats. I didn't know any girls who did back then, though it was one of the few jobs in town. Instead, I left Haines as soon as I could. But where I went to school, back East, I did not fit in. There were too many people crowded into airless classrooms and streets. Homesickness lay like a constant, dry weight on my heart until it seemed that there was no place for me anywhere. And the tension between wanting to belong there and wanting to move on never went away.

My own family seemed like permanent strangers then, even in Haines, isolated both by habit and by background. My father had been raised back East—Catholic, white, and middle class. He ran away to Alaska and became a fisherman. Now I think he never meant to stay. He was only looking for a season's glamour before beginning his real life. But the years passed, responsibilities piled up season by season: four children in the end, on a deckhand's income. Soon it was too late to go. Bright dreams come and after a while they go, quick as fireworks, and there you are, holding only ashes, a burned stick, wondering how time went by so fast. And it—the ocean—must have been nothing like what he imagined, as it was nothing like it for me now. It was always a little harder than expected: hard on bodies and hard on families, too.

I remember seeing my mother sit in our sunlit pickup truck, counting money into the lap of her denim skirt before she went into the grocery store. She looked up and saw my dad coming toward us unexpectedly, home early from fishing. She jumped out of the truck and ran toward him, dollar bills flying like birds out of her hands, uncounted. They were so joyful then, before life twisted them apart.

We called him some nights on the marine operator, the call passing through Kodiak and heard by all the boats on their radios. Fishermen listened as other men's wives and girlfriends talked of home troubles: the money spent too quickly, the truck broken down. And sometimes a sound crept into their voices that let the others know it wouldn't be long now before the calls quit coming. Or they heard the silence on the far end of the line, as two people struggled to find common language but could not. It must have seemed that there were too many troubles faced alone with the other far away, too many days my mother spent stranded in a lonely cabin, with four kids and no neighbors nearby, too many nights with him far out at sea.

Now, I loved my family, but I did not want to go back to the life that seemed to be laid out for women there. To stay home while the man went fishing seemed like a trap, but I could not yet imagine myself at sea. When I left school I began to wander.

The winter I turned twenty-three I traveled north. I took a job in Fairbanks at the Golden Eagle Saloon. It was a small place at the edge of town where few people went and where they paid me under the table in crumpled bills. I liked the mindless, active motion of tending bar for a time. But soon there were nights when the bar, with the shacks outside and the dirty snow of half-urban Alaska, seemed like a familiar trap itself. I'd lock the door after the last customer left, scrub the beer-sticky tables, and feel that my life was going nowhere. *I don't belong here*, I thought. I'd been looking for the wilderness, not bars to tend in the backwoods towns where I grew up.

The night I quit it was ten below, cold for March, even in Fairbanks. I dumped another shovelful of coal into the bar stove, scooped up the ashes, and carried them outside to shake over the icy path to the door.

Five men sat together at the bar, each hunched over a dollar-a-glass draft of Miller. Ed was halfway through his favorite Vietnam story: "It was my first night in camp, and I could hear screaming. I lay in the tent listening and shitting my pants. Come to find out next morning, there were a bunch of snakes around there. They weren't poisonous, but they'd drop out of the trees onto guys taking a piss. Put the fear of Christ in us all."

None of the other men paid much attention. Andy folded a dollar bill into the shape of a swan, his pudgy fingers moving with careful deliberation. He was already drunk. When he finished he flapped its wings and tossed it over to me.

"Set me up another one, won't you, nurse?"

At the far end of the bar, a man sat alone drinking Full Sail. I didn't recognize him, but I liked his blue eyes and the way he sat quietly, staring out the window as he drank. It was a dark night, and the window had become a mirror of the room, a mirror that held within its depths the shadows of the dogs outside the bar and, inside that, the narrow face of the man himself. To me, he looked different from the rest, already cloaked in a kind of specialness.

More men came in, strangers. They looked me up and down as they ordered their drinks. Self-conscious now, I moved behind the bar, knowing their eyes followed me despite the deliberate shabbiness of my worn jeans and flannel shirt. I was blonde, dizzy, and a little drunk. As I bent over the cooler, filled glasses, and pushed back my hair, I felt as though they held me prisoner with the blunt, hot force of their watchfulness.

The bar grew crowded, noisy. Still, the one man sat alone, looking out the window.

"What do you see?" I asked him after he had been sitting for an hour without speaking. As if it might be different from what I, or the rest of us, saw.

"Nothing real," he answered with a smile.

I held out my hand. "My name is Rosemary."

"What?"

"Rosemary."

"You look tired, Rosemary," he tried out my name.

"I'm not allowed to be tired," I said. I liked him. We talked again over the next hour, whenever I had a moment of slack time between customers. He said his name was Nate. He was a commercial fisherman and would be running a boat come April.

"How odd!" I said. "Oh, hang on . . ." Someone at the end of the bar had pushed his glass forward for another drink. I hurried to fill it, then another. When I returned to Nate he was waiting to hear the end of my thought.

"Why odd?" he asked, his eyebrows lifted.

"It's just a coincidence. I'm leaving here next week and going north, once halibut season opens there, to look for a job fishing or in a cannery."

"You're leaving town? Why?"

"No reason," I tried to explain. "I want to go out on the ocean, to know what it's like out there," I said at last, hoping he would understand what I could not articulate. "I want to get out of here."

I was thinking of the coast, of what I'd had and left. The smell of March by the ocean, and the longing I'd always had to slip past the horizon of the sea. In the forest behind my parents' cabin I'd built a hideout in the top of a spruce tree full of crows. From the highest branches I could see far out over the water; see the wind coming, chasing patterns on the sea; and see the storms slip past our sheltered inlet. Sometimes boats would cross the horizon, though they rarely came near to land here. The crows whirled up in black and scattered gusts, gulls balanced on the wind, and the sea ducks drove out over the water in quick lines, their wings singing as they passed. I wanted all of it again, the tree itself, the ocean, and to be farther out to sea than I had ever been. But how can you say that in a crowded, shabby bar to a man you just met who is already growing drunk?

Nate looked at me closely. "I see," he said. "Do you have a piece of paper and a pen?"

I handed him the bar pen and a bit of cardboard torn from an empty Marlboro carton. He wrote something on it, clutching the pen. "That's the number for the *Antagonizer*, the boat I'll be running. Call me this summer if you need a job. I might not be able to help you out, but it's worth a shot."

"The *Antagonizer*? That's a good name for a boat."

"Mark, the guy who owns it, he's got two other boats, the *Relentless* and the *Shameless*. I always thought those names suited him. Mark's a strange man." Nate's face lit up as he told me about his work. I leaned toward him as I listened. Strange names jangled like music in his tales: Egegik. Togiak. Bristol Bay. Each one enticed me, if only because it sounded so far away.

A crowd of snowmachiners pulled up outside. Five of them crowded through the door together. I hurried to the taps and was busy for some time pouring their drinks. I had one eye on Nate, wanting to talk, but before I could go back to him he got up to leave. He was taller than I'd thought, and drunker. He stumbled as he headed for the door. I stared after him, strangely disappointed.

"Hey, Blondie," Andy called. "Have you forgotten about me?" Breaking out of my thoughts, I hurried to pour him another drink. As I did, I glanced down the line of men that sat against the bar. I saw how glum they were and how they stared, unmoving, at the TV, only their eyes alive. That night I locked the door knowing that I would not stay there much longer. My life was going to change. It had to.

Now I stood knee-deep in fish on a steel boat, far from the warm illusions of the bar. It was little more than a momentary dream that sent me back to coastal Alaska, but I was glad I'd followed it. Here, I thought, where everyone else is as eccentric as I am and the restless water sings to us all, I might find what I'm looking for. It was the sea itself that held me fascinated, as it held so much human flotsam eddying along its shores.

The man from Fort Yukon picked up our conversation again as

though there had been no pause. "Yeah. I know a lot of Bonnie Jameses. Which Bonnie James would that be? Would that be the one with the baby?"

"I don't know if she has a baby now. She's about my age. A real sweet girl, pretty, with crooked teeth. She went to school with my sister up in Fairbanks, that's how I met her," I said.

He thought for a moment as we both pitched fish.

"I think that would be the younger Bonnie," he said finally. "I don't know her so well, but I know her family better. It's been a long time since I went back to Fort Yukon."

"Why'd you leave?" I asked him abruptly. "If it's not rude to ask."

The man smiled and shrugged. I realized then how unhealthy he looked, thinner than anything human should be, with the cramped teeth and yellowish skin of malnutrition. "Things happen. I'll go back, though, someday," he said, and smiled again the sweet, happy smile of a dreamer. "You going back home someday?"

"Someday." Maybe someday I'd go back to a lot of things. Here in the boat's hold, I missed my home.

As we got farther down in the bins the work grew harder. We were stooping now, groping for fish in the sea of loose ice that slid across the floor. My gloves had soaked through long since and my hands ached so with the cold that they could hardly close around the fish. When the hold was empty I didn't know what time it was or how long I'd been working. I climbed up to the dock into darkness.

"Come back in the morning," the foreman said. "We'll pay you then, and there might be another boat for you to unload, too."

"Thanks," I said. I rinsed off my gear at the faucet with the rest of the crew, handed it back to the foreman, and walked away, back to the ordinary winter town.

FOUR

⌒

THREE NIGHTS AFTER I left the *Arctic Storm*, I heard my name as I passed the Salty Dawg. I looked back. A small, thin man hurried after me. His walk had something hopeful, almost jaunty, in it, but his face looked tired under its graying stubble.

"Buy you a drink and we'll talk about a job," he called. The skipper of the *Arctic Storm* came out behind him, shouting, "Damn you, Jay, you're stealing my deckhand. You're gonna work for me, aren't you, sweetheart?"

I let myself be herded inside, strangely elated at the thought of fishing again.

"What'll you have?" Jay asked. He hooked his feet around the barstool, spread his bony elbows, and tilted his head at me. His eyes shone. "You'd rather work for me, wouldn't you, sweetie? I got a lot better boat than Don here. Lot better." He winked. "My other deckhand is healthy, too."

"I'll have a Rainier," I said. It was what they were drinking. "Thanks. But I think Don has first dibs."

"Nope. He doesn't. He's fooling you. He doesn't even have a crew lined up."

"Yeah, Jay's bought you a drink," Don conceded. "Guess you're

31

working for him." A sour look spread over his plump face. "I haven't found a replacement for Everett, anyhow. He fucking bailed on me, left me with my ass hanging out in the wind. That's the last time I go bail for a fucking deckhand."

"Leave him in the drunk tank next time," Jay advised.

The bartender set my beer in front of me, along with a shot of peppermint schnapps and a mug of tepid hot chocolate. I raised an eyebrow.

"That's from that guy," she said, and pointed down the bar.

"Oh, yeah, he always buys those for women. Must've known it to work one time," Jay said. He leaned over my shoulder and poured the schnapps into the mug for me. "Hey, did I tell you I gave Everett a ride out the road that day you guys came back in? He claimed he was heading for Anchorage."

"Bet he never did go to a doctor," Don said.

"Hell, there wasn't anything wrong with him except he was coming down off a month-long binge. You were lucky he didn't get the DTs on the boat," Jay said. "You know, I asked him why he was quitting, and he said, 'There's a woman on the boat.' I said, 'Well, Everett, what did she do? Did she hit on you?' but he just kept saying 'She's a woman,' like that explained it all." He laughed at the look on my face. "Some guys are like that—if something goes wrong, it's the woman's fault. Can't hardly blame them. I wouldn't hire you myself if I wasn't desperate."

"She's a girl, but she's a good worker," Don said. "Weighs about as much as a goddamn Pomeranian, but she's got enough grit for a two-hundred-pounder."

Jay waved for the bartender and ordered fresh drinks. I tried to catch her eye to refuse, but she slid another shot in my direction.

A man spoke from down the bar. "That the girl took a job with you, Don?"

"Yeah."

"All of us on the *Totem*, we had bets on how long she'd stick around. Nobody thought she'd last more than ten minutes."

"She did okay. God knows I didn't think so when I hired her. Just couldn't find anybody else."

"Get her a drink," the man told the bartender. She grabbed a shot glass, poured it full, and slapped it down to join the two in front of me. I shook my head, but she looked past me, indifferently. Trapped, I gulped the last of the first shot and started on the second. I was still hurt at Everett's words. I'd thought he liked me, and the thought had helped, but now it seemed I'd been mistaken. I thought of him standing by the road, and I wondered why he left. It seemed like there was nowhere else for him to go. Or maybe he knew that he was trapped, too. Maybe that was why.

Uneasily, I pulled back from my thoughts.

"My name's Doug," the man from the *Totem* introduced himself. "So, did you make any money?"

Don caught my eye and shook his head.

I said, "We had to come back early because of Everett."

"Oh, yeah, I heard about that. Season's tapering off, anyway. We didn't put in more than a few hundred pounds ourselves last trip. Figure we'll haul our gear in pretty soon."

"The *Totem* always does better than anyone else," Jay told me, as though warning me not to expect too much from him.

"We do okay," Doug said. "We got our pots way down in the entrance. Fishing's good, but the weather's just snotty. And the cost of fuel takes a big bite out of our check."

I took another sip of schnapps and hot chocolate and washed it down with a gulp of beer. It tasted foul, but I didn't want to hurt anyone's feelings. I looked at the men. They were looking at the bar, at the bottles behind it, and at the bartender's backside. I picked up my glass, cupped it hidden in my hands against my knees, and poured it out onto the sawdust floor. The liquid disappeared.

Jay tapped the bar for another round. "We need to celebrate me hiring the best-looking deckhand in Homer." The bartender handed me another shot. Defeated, I stood up to go.

"Which boat's yours?" I asked Jay.

"The *American Eagle*. It's tied up along the transient float." Don laughed at that, but Jay ignored him. "We'll head out at four in the morning. You going to get your gear?"

"Yeah. Okay if I sleep on the boat tonight?"

"Yeah. I just hired another deckhand, name of Scott. He's green too, but I'll teach you guys. He'll be on the boat tonight as well."

"All right." I turned away. The room swayed around me as I made for the door. I heard the men laughing as I grabbed the door too hard and almost lost my balance.

Outside, the evening was growing dark. Snow fell, blanketing the water and blotting out the far reaches of Kachemak Bay. As I slid down the ramp, steep with low tide, I heard the flat, detached tones of the weather recording come on outside the harbor master's.

Southwest winds to fifteen knots, becoming west twenty before midnight. Seas ten feet, building to twelve feet by morning. Rain and fog.

I hunched my shoulders, feeling cold and scared. The *American Eagle* lay at the foot of the ramp. A blue, steel-hulled boat, forty feet long with a high wheelhouse and a long, low-railed back deck. Its sides seeped rust under a bloom of worn-out paint. I pounded on the door but no one answered, so I walked in and lay down on a bunk, pushing aside a pile of magazines. The cabin was windowless, walled with steel, with only one door through which the yellow dock lights shone. Maybe it was because of that that I couldn't sleep. I felt as if I were lying in a jail, and the narrow bunk with its flat, hard, sticky mattress did not help.

After a while I got back up and went on deck. The moon was rising, and the last light was dying from the west in a faint, wintry glow. On the next boat over two men talked quietly. Their voices, echoing out over the water, had a lonely sound. I stood looking across the harbor. The tide was coming in, and the boats shifted restlessly at their moorings. Streams of foam ran along their sides.

The water shifted before my eyes, swelling vastly under the fabric of boats. I shivered, afraid in a way I couldn't name.

Inside again, I lay back down, staring at the ceiling and the surface of the upper bunk. Someone had drawn on it in pencil, a picture of fish and of the boat itself, but the pencil marks had nearly faded out. After a while I fell into a doze. Hours slid by. Past two o'clock, the door creaked open. A man stepped on board. I woke up fully as he slung his duffel bag into the bunk opposite mine. A heavy man, with a round, dark face.

"Name's Scott," he said when he saw my eyes were open. "I don't know squat about fishing."

"Neither do I," I answered, watching him. "I've only been out once before, on the *Arctic Storm*."

"I came down to look at this one after I got the job," he said. "It looked like shit, but then I saw the *Arctic Storm* and I thought, 'Well at least I'm not on that one.'"

"Yeah, I think this will be better," I said. "Those guys were kind of marginal at best."

He kept on without really listening, "Course, what did you think of those low rails on the deck? Seems like a wave could come right over that, sweep us off the deck?"

We stared at each other, mutually imagining it.

"Don't say things like that," he said at last, forgetting the words had been his own. He stowed his gear with nervous care and lay down.

We lapsed into silence until the engine roared to life below us. Jay shouted into the fo'c'sle to make sure we were awake. "Time to go kill fish!"

We followed him on deck. It was cold outside, and dark, the glare of cannery lights reflecting over the slick black water. We cast off, coiled the lines, and stood shivering as the *American Eagle* slipped out of the harbor, watching the land fall away behind us.

"Can you fix some coffee, Rose? Maybe some breakfast?" Jay called down. It appeared that, as the woman, this would always be my task. I went back into the cabin, started coffee, and found some bacon and eggs. As I put the bacon on to fry the boat began rocking to a gentle swell.

When I stepped on deck again, carrying Jay's breakfast, a thin pink line had begun to color the east. Far behind us, the lights of town disappeared from sight. I climbed the ladder to the wheelhouse, kicked the door open, and set down the food. Scott and Jay sat silently together, watching the dawn in a wheelhouse choked with cigarette smoke.

"Bacon and eggs. My favorite." Jay grinned at me as if I'd brought him Christmas on a plate. I sat down next to Scott on the day bunk and looked around.

"Sure is pretty," Jay said, gesturing with an eggy fork. "One thing about fishing, you got the best views in the world. Those big shots in cities? They couldn't pay to see this."

Steadily, the nearest mountains took shape and substance out of the dark. Across the inlet, peaks began to glow with approaching light. The sky took fire, which spread quickly and died out as the sun came up. Wind stirred the water, fanning shadows across its slow swells. The cold air made the surface smoke. I left the wheelhouse and stood on deck to watch. Outside, it smelled of dawn and water.

Scott came down the ladder behind me. He said nothing, just stood spitting over the side, his lip full of Copenhagen, looking ill at ease.

"Brr-rr," he said at last. "'S cold out here. You don't get seasick, huh? I was worried, but I ain't sick yet." He hitched his pants up, spat, and went inside.

I cleaned the galley and lay down. The sun was high before we reached Jay's pots. When we found the first, Jay came down on deck to show us how to pull it. He hooked the buoy and passed the line through the block, a pulley that spooled the line aboard. I ran the hydraulics, keeping a hand on the lever to keep the block turning while Scott coiled the incoming line. When the pot broke the surface of the water, Scott swung it inboard. I grabbed the other side, and we hauled it over the rail.

It was blowing by then, a westerly chop, and the boat pitched underfoot. I tried to gauge its motion, to use its sway to land the pot on deck. But it wasn't easy. The pot swung in. We flung ourselves against it as it crashed to a standstill on the launcher and yanked it open, releasing a mass of life: gray cod—their sides gleaming like wet gunmetal—starfish, seashells, crabs with seaweed growing on their backs, halibut, red bladder wrack, and ribbon kelp. The second pot held the same and an octopus, too.

Jay cursed from overhead when he saw the octopus. "Those fuckers will run your string and clean you out. But don't pitch it," he warned us, "I know a guy who'll buy them all."

I sprawled on deck to wrestle it free and hung it from a noose the way he told me. The cod we bled and threw into the hold. Everything else we tossed over the side as we scrabbled for smashed and broken fish.

Once the pot was empty Scott crawled inside. He fumbled the snap on the bait jar, and I fumbled when I latched it shut after he crawled out. The deck was slippery with a coat of blood, blood covered our hands, and the unfamiliar work tired us in body and mind. We braced ourselves and heaved both pots over the side again, and already we were on to the next pot.

"Bag's on the rail," Jay shouted, Scott bent to hook it and slip it through the block. This time I coiled while he brought in the line. We hardly spoke. I had nothing to say. He had nothing to say. There was only the mindless, dizzying, almost pointless, and brutal work and our own clumsy bodies and frozen hands. The waves kept coming; the pots kept coming.

Jay quit early that day—partly out of pity and partly from disgust at a green crew—and took us behind the island to anchor for the night. We had only caught a few cod, but he told us that was unusual.

"It'll be different tomorrow," he said. "Tomorrow we'll all be getting rich. Right, Rose?"

He'd kept a halibut for our dinner. I cut it up and fried it on the oil stove. We gulped our food, sopping up the juice with stale bread. My hands were seamed with salt and cold. One thumb bled from under the nail where the pot had struck it. But that was at least a minor injury, compared to all that might have happened. I thought of that, and I thought, too, of the octopus we'd killed and the other creatures swept over the side. Even I knew what we'd done was wrong. Octopuses were protected, and Jay's friend must be buying under the table. But I didn't yet have the nerve to speak up.

Even so, the cod fishing had somehow begun to seem more honest than buying food in a store. In the past when I'd purchased my food, its clean, bright packaging had seemed to absolve me of guilt. But now, the reality of killing to eat made me tired and ill.

I sat watching the men eat steadily and silently, as if eating, too, were a job. Their bodies seemed distorted by work. I remembered my father.

"But what do you do when you're gone out there, Dad?" I'd asked him once.

"I dance," he once told me. "I'm a dancer in the old, dumb, broke-down guys' polka." And I pictured them up there in the North, stamping their feet and twirling, all the heavy, saggy men he worked with abruptly transformed. *Dancers*, I thought. Someday I'd see them. I knew by then something closer to the truth, but when I imagined him that summer, I still thought of him dancing to music I was too far away to hear, a small figure jerking and twisting in a fading crowd of people and fish and whales.

By then he was absent from home for months at a time, following the fishing season. In those days, I remembered him best as a series of letters written on yellow paper in a cramped hand. He wrote about whales and birds and dawns he'd seen, but never about being homesick or lonely. He'd left that for me to find out for myself.

Now, without finishing my dinner, I went on deck again and scraped my meal over the side. I wondered if anyone really knew how much damage we were doing to the earth, or how long it could last. There seemed to be no escaping it.

The next day we started fishing before dawn. Jay had a string of gear far offshore, in deep water toward Mount Augustine. We bucked our way out to it in morning chop. A strong, fresh breeze whistled across the deck, carrying spray that smacked against our bow. Scott and I ground bait as we headed out, and the cold breeze shocked our drowsy bodies awake. I watched the light rise, touching distant mountains and the vivid sea.

Ahead, Jay's buoys beaded the water. I grabbed the buoy hook and leaned over the rail, caught the line, and slipped it in the block. Scott hit the lever, our bodies tuned now to each other's motions.

The line coiled for me more fluidly than it had before. But the first pot we hauled was empty. A few bones lay in the bottom.

"That fucker. Octopus did that," Jay said again. "Sometimes one of those guys will run your whole fucking string, eat everything in it. They can always get in and out if you give 'em time," he fumed, as if the octopus had no right to exist.

I looked away. I didn't think the octopus was all that we could blame for our failure. Octopus or no, our pots were empty, and though the sea was beautiful, it seemed empty, too. Our catch was thin and the men were bitter. We ran the string of gear all morning, and still our hold held little more than a yellowish broth of bloody water.

And though that night Jay told us he was raising our crew shares, Scott didn't thank him. He'd worked it out, as had I.

"So, you mean I made ten bucks instead of five, is that it?" he said.

Jay shrugged and scraped his plate. "We'll get 'em. Right, Rose?" he said.

Scott stood up, lit a cigarette, and dragged on his rain jacket. "Going to gut those slimy bastards," he said.

I kicked my boots on and followed him. There were six of them, octopuses hanging together like tired balloons. They were illegal and yet were all we had caught that was worth money. I took one down and sat spraddled in my rain gear on the deck, the octopus between my legs. Its head lay in my lap and its tentacles spread limp across the deck, shifting to the motion of the boat. In death it had turned a dull, mottled purple.

"How do I gut it?" I asked.

"Just turn its head inside out and cut out its insides. I'll show you." Scott untied another octopus. His bad mood seemed to have passed over. "Jay showed me last night while you were cooking." He sat down beside me, holding his own octopus. "You find the edge of the hood," Scott said as he demonstrated. "See how there's just this little bit of membrane holding it on? Cut that. Now feel along the sides—there are two more membranes like the first. When you cut those, you can peel back the hood." He had severed the soft tissue as he talked and peeled the hood off inside out. A pile of organs neatly encased in clear film rolled from the body.

"Try not to bust the bag of guts. All you have to do now is to cut it away at the beak and your octopus is clean." He lifted the organs free, hefted them in his hand like a football, and pitched them over the side. Seagulls gathered in the clear air.

"Strange," I said.

"Yeah," he said. "They say they're as smart as dogs, too. I wouldn't know." He shrugged, his head bent to the job.

I looked down at the octopus in my lap and cut through its skin, severing the membranes and releasing its inner parts. They fell between my legs, bright with blood. I threw them away, set aside what remained, and gathered in another octopus. As I cut into the second one, it began to move. Its foot came up and twisted around mine. For a moment, I thought I would be sick.

"Sucker's still alive," Scott commented. "Last night one of those little bastards went for my goolies. I was like 'Oh! Oh! Oh! Get offa me!' but you can't get those suckers off when they want to hang on."

I stared at him. He kept cutting, talking, watching it move. "I tore his brains out and that slowed him down, or my girlfriend would've been sorry when I come home."

"You can't blame it for that. What an awful way to go, gutted alive," I said. My hands were shaking with something close to fear.

"Well, we've all got to eat. Octopus gut cod alive, so to speak. You want to watch out for that beak. It'll fuck you up bad."

I hesitated. He glanced at me. "We got to eat," he said again. "Life's tough like that."

I clasped the knife again and kept on cutting, feeling troubled, sick, tired, and confused.

FIVE

⌒

OUR THIRD DAY out we fished until dark. As the sun went down, Jay called us on deck.

"Wanna run back to town?" he asked.

"Yeah!" I said, and Scott cheered up at once. We needed to sell our catch, but more than that, we were all eager to see town again.

When we reached the harbor we tied up in the slip. We would not deliver our fish until the morning. Jay went to the bar. I walked to the payphone to call Nate. I told myself I needed to talk to someone about fishing, someone who understood what it was like. But the truth was I missed him, though I hadn't heard from him since I left Fairbanks. I thought just the sound of his voice would make me feel better.

He didn't pick up. I let the phone ring to the end, hung up unhappily when the answering machine kicked on, changed my mind, and dialed once more, planning to leave a message. This time Nate answered. He'd been working on his truck and had heard his phone ring over and over. What was going on?

I mumbled an inaudible excuse and told him I'd gotten a job without giving details. He said he was rebuilding the hydraulics on the boat he was working on. Then there was nothing more to say.

The closeness we'd felt seemed to have burned away when I told him I would not stay in Fairbanks. I hung up and headed for the bar, angry with myself for being unable to talk to him easily, however much I wanted to. I wished I hadn't called, almost.

Jay was sitting on a stool near the door. He nodded as I came in, continuing his story.

"Back then, I used to have a little double-ender. Go out in the morning, load 'er up. Sell the fish. That was back before the oil spill, back in the day . . ."

But no one listened. After a time he let the story fall and looked up.

"This is my deckhand, Rose," he said. "Best-looking deckhand in the fleet."

The men nodded and turned their heads away, looking over their beers at the wall. Jay did not notice. He ordered me a drink. I did not refuse, though too many had already gone his way.

He propped his head up, peering blurrily at me.

"She's little, but she can outwork your crew," he said. "She's got more balls than any guy in here."

The man beside him looked at me and didn't answer. I thought, *I must look like a kid to him.*

"I'm telling you, Rose can outwork your crew any day," Jay insisted louder. "Tell you what, we'll make a bet on it. Most pots hauled, one day. My crew against yours."

"That's stupid, Jay," one of the men said quietly. "That's the way to get somebody hurt."

Jay blustered, then subsided, staring at his glass. The bar grew crowded and the temperature rose. The men settled into talking about work. There weren't many cod around this year, they agreed. You couldn't hardly catch enough to make bait at forty cents a pound.

"You guys on the *Totem*, you do pretty good though, huh?" one said. "Bill's a damn good skipper. Fucker must be part cod. He can find fish when no one else can."

"I heard you got pencil-whipped bad though," someone else joined in.

"Yeah," the man from the *Totem* agreed. "We caught some fish, but when you take out for food and fuel there ain't much left of a check. First time I ever got charged for crane use, too."

The bartender came past us, grabbing empty glasses, looking for a nod from each man, and bringing each a fresh drink in response. Each time she passed, someone ordered me a beer, and in keeping up, I was becoming drunk.

"Busy in here tonight," someone said. "It's the guys back from crabbing."

"I heard they wrecked the bar in Dutch the night crabbing closed . . ." the *Totem* man said. When he finished his story the next man tried to top it.

"Do you remember the year they lost the *St. George*, and the guys afterward drew a line of cocaine down the bar? The whole length of it. Worst night I ever spent."

I sat silent, staring at the bar. It was brass, rubbed to a shine by the elbows of men who had rested against it in sweat shirts and flannels and Carhartt coats. Worn dollar bills covered the ceiling, each pinned in place with a red thumbtack. Men had signed them and written their hometowns on them, but the dust and smoke had worn their names away.

Behind me the men were laughing, but I couldn't join them. After only two trips out, I had nothing to say. Instead, I listened, loneliness waiting somewhere outside. My head drooping, I tried to fix my mind on the stories that swelled and returned on the flood of talk drifting through the bar like currents, as if they themselves could rescue me, give me a history and place to belong. But my thoughts seemed to skate over an abyss. I was looking for adventure because I felt like I belonged nowhere, and I didn't know why that was so. It seemed as though I did not, could not, fit into the world, though I listened to the men and remembered what they said.

Once I traveled with my father down the Coleen River, looking for a cabin where a friend of his, Charlie Wolf, had once lived—in the old days, before Alaska changed with the pipeline. Charlie'd gotten sick one winter and had to leave, not knowing that he would never return. Not long afterward he passed away. Now Dad wanted to see if he could find his cabin, as if, maybe, it would make some difference, call back the days when he was young and Charlie was his friend.

We did not find it, though we searched and searched. In the end, we understood that it must have burned down so long ago that running green grass and fireweed had covered over the remaining logs; burned, and no one even knew. I remember the look on my dad's face as he kicked at the earth, trying to find a place that had vanished long ago. It was as if a world had gone with it, and we were left empty-handed on the riverbank.

Later, out in the current again, we saw flotsam piled along the banks. It seemed to move as we passed, and he told me a word, *parallax*. It describes the apparent motion of an object, whose position changes only because you yourself have passed it by. Parallax. He watched the bank, where no one stood, as if his own young self faded out of sight.

I thought I knew a little how he'd felt, trying to hang on to a vanishing perspective as the world slipped past too quickly, erasing us. I didn't know if the stories I heard were true. It didn't matter. The hows and whys of any story were rapidly washed away by passing days. What was left was a question of identity. For the men, stories were a way of claiming who they were, of participating in a history that was, like all history, shaped by myth. They were also a way of marking time when there was nowhere else to go.

But the men began to fall silent. After a time the spell broke. I left the Salty Dawg and headed to the boat. The harbor was dark but for the stark yellow glare reflected over the water from the fish dock. It was raining hard, and when I stepped into the cabin I saw that the rain had leaked through the roof above, pooling on the table and floor. I slid into my bunk wishing I hadn't spent the night getting drunk. But I was from out of town and had nowhere to go but the bar.

At four in the morning Jay woke me. We headed out. His eyes were rimmed with red, and he looked old in the harsh light of the cabin. I made a pot of coffee and took some up to him as he steered out into the bay. He thanked me. "Getting too old to be staying out late drinking like a kid," he said, trying to make a joke of his hangover. But he and I both knew that as soon as we returned to port he'd head straight up to the Salty Dawg. For Jay, too, there was nowhere else to go.

SIX

⌁

APRIL PASSED. We kept fishing, moving our pots as the cod moved into fresh waters. I learned how to mend the pots, how to coil and steer. The days grew longer, and we caught more fish, though still hardly enough to pay for fuel. One day I realized I'd begun to love going out to sea, the hard, fresh wind and the way the dawn broke over the water. But at the same time, I had no intention of staying past the spring. This life was too harsh for me. It seemed bearable, even exciting, for a time only because I knew it was temporary. In my mind, there was still some wider ocean farther along. The soul of adventure is its brief life.

Scott, though, came to hate fishing wholeheartedly.

"Fuck this shit," he cursed under his breath morning after morning. As the days passed he grew more and more sullen. Jay avoided his eyes and seemed to look to me for approval. *Strange for a skipper to seek approval from a green deckhand,* I thought. It was as if he needed someone to believe in him in the face of his continuing failure to find fish. Most of the other boats had quit by then. But he kept on.

"Means more fish and higher prices for us," he said, though we now knew that was not true.

Things came to a breaking point on a day in late April. We

hauled pots until late in the afternoon, most of them empty of cod. We didn't stop for breakfast or lunch but kept on working, hauling, checking, resetting each barren pot until the tide rose high enough to stop us.

At four in the afternoon, Jay gave the word that it would be an hour before we could fish again. I walked into the cabin and grabbed the cookie bag without even taking off my gloves.

It was empty.

That bastard, I thought, irrationally. *I bet he's got handfuls of them stashed up in the wheelhouse.* I tore off my gloves, opened the refrigerator, and grabbed the cheese.

Scott came in, opened a can of vienna sausages, and swallowed them in handfuls.

"God, these things are gross," he said. "Want some?" He thumbed another out of the can.

I shook my head.

He shrugged and threw the can into the trash. "I wish to hell we had something decent to eat," he said.

"I know," I said. But I gulped down the cheap, bad food that was all we had, until I was nauseated, then put the cheese back in the fridge. It was moldy, but we might want it anyway. I lay down in my bunk, almost despairing.

Two hours later Jay came down from the wheelhouse.

"All right, guys," he said. "With this next string I want you to stack the pots on deck. We're gonna call it a season."

He looked us straight in the eye with the calmness of defeat. "What you'll do, just get the fish out of the pot same as always. Instead of puckering it up again, leave it open. We'll get the picking hook on it, drag it back across the deck, and tie it off standing upright. I'll show you how. We can get about a dozen pots on board, then we'll head into town, come on back out in the morning, and pick up another load."

Scott and I stared at him.

He shrugged. "Hell of a season, huh?" he said, and closed the door.

"I'm glad he figured out it was quitting time," Scott said. "Thought he was gonna keep on looking for imaginary fish until he died of old age. Hell, I was about ready to quit on my own without waiting for Jay's say-so."

"Wonder what he's gonna do now?" I said. I worried about Jay. "Seems like he might have a hard time finding a job."

"Go on back to shore and bum drinks from other broke cod fishermen." Scott gave me an unpleasant look. "I don't know why I thought he'd be a good skipper, why I took a job with him in the first place."

I kicked my gear on and went out on deck. It had grown colder while we were inside, and the wind had freshened. We waited as the boat moved slowly up on a string of pots.

"Bag's on the rail!" Jay hollered. Scott hooked the buoy as we slid alongside it. I took over the hydraulics, bringing it in. Jay came down the ladder behind me, tapped my shoulder, and gestured for me to step aside. He shoved the lever forward, sending the block spinning at full speed. Scott glanced up, startled, struggling with the line. In a moment he was far behind. The incoming line looped itself unguided in a pile. Jay stopped the block and waited grimly, then slammed the lever forward again.

"You gonna run the block that fast, line's gonna get tangled," Scott said.

"You coiled that line the way I showed you, you'd be able to keep up with the block. Lemme show you again." Jay stopped the block and reached to take the line. Scott stared at him angrily, then dropped his eyes. He handed Jay the line and moved to run the hydraulics himself.

Scott opened up the block full speed, but Jay kept pace with it, his hands moving in a slow parabola that sent the line settling at his feet. Jay coiled in a dancing rhythm, bringing the line in gently over his right hand while his left hand held it. When his arm was fully extended, he threw a loop into the line he held, dropped it at his feet, and took hold again.

"Told you, you don't need to go hand over hand," he said. "Just do like this."

Scott took over coiling again. For a moment he tried to imitate Jay, but the motions didn't make sense to him. He kept on struggling hand over hand. Sweat flew from his forehead, but he couldn't keep up. Almost imperceptibly, Jay eased off the speed so that he wouldn't fall behind again. "You'll get the hang of it," he consoled Scott. "Took me a long time to learn, and you know? I ain't even very good. Some of those guys are artists."

The pot came up. We brought it in and took out the single fish. Scott slipped the picking hook into the rim. Together we lifted the front edge off the launcher to the deck. Jay raised the picking hook so that the pot rose. Upended, it towered over my head.

"Get it back in the far corner," Jay said. Scott and I half dragged, half guided it while Jay ran the hydros. I moved with it, heaving it forward, trying to take advantage of the motion of the water. Scott strained on the other side, swearing monotonously as he pushed.

I heard Jay shout. The pot swung toward me. An echoing clang shook the deck as it slammed down where I'd been standing. I must've jumped back, but I didn't remember it.

There was a moment of silence.

Then, "Hook slipped out," Jay said briefly. "Get it back in, and make sure it's in good." He lowered the hook into Scott's hands. Scott fastened it back to the pot, and slowly Jay raised the hook again. The pot rose with it, swinging overhead. We shoved it against the rail. I tied it off with shaking hands.

With the next cod pot we hauled, it happened again. The hook came loose and the pot fell. This time Jay shut off the hydraulics and came forward to help us lift it back up by hand. "You guys think you can handle these pots without the hook?" he asked. "I don't like having it slipping out like this."

"My mom wouldn't like it either," I said.

"We'll do like Mother says. From now on, we'll move these pots by hand."

It was heavier work without the aid of the hook. Jay ran down to help us lift each pot upright, then Scott and I flung our combined weight against the standing pot, inching it back to its place. The deck grew slippery with slime and blood. I fell to my knees, stood, and fell again. I knew that Scott was picking up slack for me, and I tried to apologize. "I'm sorry," I said. "I wish I could do more." He looked at me and shrugged. "It's not your fault," he said. "You're just not big enough."

"You're not a man," he added.

Stricken, I looked away. Slowly, we stacked eleven pots, four along one rail, five on the other, and two upright in the center. A stack of buoys and line filled the last of the deck space, close against the cabin door. When we finished the light was failing fast.

"Think you can rustle us up some grub, Rose?" Jay said to me. His face was carved in a mask of weariness and stress. He and Scott went up to the wheelhouse to smoke. I walked into the cabin to look for food. There was nothing left but sausage and eggs. I slapped the sausage into a pan and braced my belly against the stove to keep the pan on the burner while I broke the eggs. Scott came down when the food was ready. I sent him up again with a plate for Jay.

"Jay says thank you," he reported back.

"How many of those pots are there again?" I asked him. "Fifty?"

"Yeah, about. We've lost a few," Scott said.

"Figure, five or six days of this?"

"Yeah. And you know, we ain't even gonna make any money doing it. Man, I got job interviews to go to. I need to be on shore. Got a interview lined up at Land's End restaurant. Man, you should be a bartender. Make a lot more money than busting your ass out here."

The door swung open. Jay came in to throw his plate in the sink.

"That was great." He smiled at me, slammed the door, and was gone. I got up again to start the dishes.

"I already was a bartender once," I said. "I couldn't stand talking to people all night long. I was being paid to chitchat and flirt."

"Make great tips bartending. I made fifty dollars a night some-times last fall, just bussing when the tourists was here," Scott said.

The tips made it worse, I thought. *I'd be working for tips, being nice to assholes just so they'd give me an extra dollar. You can lose your self-respect pretty quick that way, and never know it's gone.*

Scott stood up. "Pretty soon I'm going to be off of this boat and will never take a fishing job again," he said. He headed to his bunk. By the time I finished the dishes I could hear him snoring. I sat down at the table, tired and sore, and took out Nate's picture again. I looked at it for a while, wondering if he was seeing some other girl now, then put it away and went out on deck. The seas had hollowed in thickening shadow as the low angle of the light made them seem steeper, and their faces darker. I sat down on a buoy to watch. Looking at the picture hadn't made me feel less alone. It seemed like we all wanted too much from each other. Maybe Nate and I were both looking too hard for a connection in a stranger's face.

After a while I smelled cigarette smoke and looked up. Jay was watching me. When I saw him, he nodded and stepped out of sight. I moved so that I couldn't be seen from above. I did not like it when I caught him watching me. There was a heat to his eyes that trou-bled me.

SEVEN

~~~

THAT NIGHT WE stayed in the harbor. The next morning, when Jay came to wake us, Scott was gone. His duffel was missing from the bunk.

"Looks like he quit," Jay said. "Guess we'll be staying in town today. I'll have to look around for a replacement."

Late in the evening, I returned to the boat. Scott's bunk was still empty. I fell asleep wondering what Jay would do.

At four in the morning he came to wake me. I felt his hand on my shoulder and sat up quickly. He was half-drunk, but his face was set. "Looked all day and never could find anyone to take Scott's place," he said. "But I've got to get those pots in. If you come with me, we can do it together. Otherwise, by god, I'll do it alone."

"I'm not quitting until we finish getting in the gear," I said. Still half-asleep, I kicked around for my boots. "You can't do it alone, Jay, you'll get hurt."

"I wish I could find Scott. I'd tell him you said that. He quits and the girl keeps working," Jay said, grinning bitterly. "It'll be more work with just two of us, but we'll get it done. By god, I'll make sure you get a good job after this, too. Hell, I know every damn skipper in town." He ducked into the engine room to start the boat. In a moment we left the harbor.

With the first pot, I realized what we were in for. I had never hauled gear without Scott. Now I had his job to do as well as my own, while Jay ran from the wheelhouse to the deck, both steering the boat and helping me. I'd never seen a man work as hard as he did then. He never slowed down or lost his temper, and I never saw him drunk. It was as if it was his final stab at being a successful skipper, as if he were holding back his own despair with sheer energy.

On the third day the wind began to blow. I lay in my bunk waiting to work, tossed back and forth by the water's motion. It was cold despite the engine heat. Fear of the ocean stirred in me, but I forced it back. Frightened as I was, deeper than the fear, I held the unarticulated, childish belief that danger was for other people, not me. And I could not bring myself to quit.

An hour out, I heard Jay stamp his foot on the floor of the wheelhouse overhead, signaling me. I crawled from my bunk and made my way upstairs. Inside, the wheelhouse swung like a pendulum.

"Wanted to ask you what you thought about this," Jay said. "I ain't gonna make you haul pots in this shit if you're scared."

It didn't occur to me that he might be looking for a reason to turn back. I thought about it, saying nothing. I wanted to go back, but at the same time I hated the thought of wasting the day, having to go out again. We were so close to finishing the job.

"I think the wind will die down pretty quick," he said. "On the other hand, it could last another three days. But come hell or high water, I've got to get these pots in before next week. So, in some ways, I'd like to do it now, when I know we can."

"All right," I said. I went down to the cabin. An hour passed. Overhead, Jay stamped on the floor again. I pulled my rain gear on and went out on deck. Foam streaked the surface of the water. Each swell passed slowly, seeming to diminish the size of the boat.

"Bag's on the rail," Jay shouted. A buoy slid past, now far below me, now near my head. I hooked it as it rose. The shock of its drag knocked me to my knees. Jay ran down to help me get the line through the block. He started coiling, lurching as we rolled. I steadied myself, hanging on to the hydros.

It will be bad when we land the pot, I thought, trying to convince myself. *But that will be the worst. Everything else is really no different from how it always has been.*

The pot broke through the surface and struck the boat. It swayed below us, still half-underwater. Jay moved to steady it. But he couldn't hold it.

"Bring it in slow," he shouted. "Use the motion . . . just like I've always told you, just like . . . just like . . ." The pot swung inboard and crashed on deck, the boat staggered, knocked broadside to the swell. I realized that we could capsize, thrown off balance by the pots, or be knocked down and unable to right the boat. But it seemed too late to turn back now. There was nothing I could do except keep working.

We tied the pot down and picked up another. Jay fretted aloud that we were working too slowly, keeping the boat off balance longer than was necessary. "You've got to understand, this is a bit of a risky situation," he kept saying. "Got to keep the boat balanced or one of these waves might knock us right over." He didn't need to say it for my sake, and I think he knew that. It was as if he was trying to placate fate.

"Let's stack the lines and buoys," he said at last. "Get 'em up along the cabin, off the stern." I grabbed a load and carried them forward. The deck there was narrow and slick, but the fast-paced work numbed my mind. Even then, I only half believed we were in danger.

I got the coils up and tied the pots in place. I leaned over the side to pass the tie-up strap through the scupper. On the third try I lost my footing. I caught myself with a hand on the pot. For a moment, I thought I would be sick. My head swam. I thought, *I might have died just then.* But the numbness returned. I kept on working.

The light was failing by the time we finished work and began our long trip back to land. The boat wallowed, weighed down by the mass of pots on deck. I sat at the cabin table, tired with the work and with relief that I was still alive, too tired to do anything but stare at the peeling yellow paint of the table.

Halfway to the harbor, Jay called me up into the wheelhouse. He said he was going to try jigging for cod once he quit pot fishing. Jigging was open for another month. It was easy work, he said, just taking fish off the hooks and keeping an eye on the machines. He'd pay me 10 percent if I wanted to come.

"I'll think about it, okay?" I said.

"Take your time," he said. "Anyhow, you can stay on the boat as long as you want."

I nodded at that but didn't answer.

When we reached the harbor, we off-loaded the pots at the fish dock and tied up in our slip. It was the same routine we had followed many times, but that day everything we did had an air of finality and defeat. We had tried pot fishing, and we had lost. We were both still broke. Even the gulls seemed to mock us. "Too bad, too bad, too bad," they cried, circling overhead. As I tied up the boat I wondered if I'd ever untie it again.

Jay disappeared into the wheelhouse. I made a sandwich and sat down at the table, still thinking over Jay's offer of a job. I didn't want to quit on him, but his plans seemed doomed to me, and I did not want to get caught up in them.

After a while he came into the galley and sat down. Our knees touched under the table. He smiled at me. His breath smelled of alcohol.

Oh hell, I thought. *Not this*. Somehow, I knew what he intended before he said a word. Something I'd hoped he'd never try.

"Looks pretty good," he said.

"It's okay," I said, looking away. "Just cheese and pickle."

"Bite?" he asked, opening his mouth. I stared at him and pushed the food across the table. He kept his mouth open, a pink hole for me to feed.

I dropped my eyes, feeling sick.

"I'm heading out," I said, and stood up, edging for the door.

"Yeah? Sure you don't want to head up to the bar with me?" His eye twitched, seeming to wink without his volition. "Buy you a cocktail."

"No. Thanks. I'll see you later."

He got up too as I tried to pass him, and moved me back against the sink, his hand on my waist. His face came too close to mine. "I'm going to go talk to a few people, see what I can find out about a market for all the cod we're going to catch jigging. You and me, we're going to get rich."

I slid out of his hands and bolted for the door. My mind wasn't working clearly. I couldn't look at him. All I could think was that I had to leave. If he were a different man, I might have hit him, but instead I felt only a wave of pity and confusion, as something I should have seen coming now overwhelmed me.

Out on the road, I hitched a ride into town. Away from the harbor I grew calmer. I didn't think Jay would have touched me at all if he hadn't thought there was already something between us. We'd forged a bond in our time on deck, but for me it was not as it was for him, and I knew I would have to leave the *American Eagle*.

Near the library, I asked to get out. As I scrambled from the seat, the driver handed me a scrap of paper with his phone number scribbled on it. I stared at it for a moment before I realized what it was. I decided he meant no harm; it was a small town, so I murmured thanks as I turned away and headed down the sidewalk. It was a Sunday evening, and the streets were all but deserted. I walked in search of a café, but when I reached one, I decided that I didn't want coffee after all. It had just been a temporary destination.

I turned and walked through the town again as a light rain began to fall. I couldn't think of where to go or what to do. I didn't know anyone who needed crew, and the thought of beginning again was daunting to me. Nor could I think of other plans. I was too broke to start over, even if I'd wanted to.

I passed the grocery store and its adjacent shops, Homer's version of a strip mall. Rainwater trickled from the gutters, and a gritty spring wind pushed trash across the parking lot. The stores were all closed, but a phone booth stood at the corner of the lot. On an impulse, I stopped to call Nate. No matter what was between us now, I wanted to talk to him. He was someone who had mattered to me and who cared what became of me, something I felt badly in need of now.

As his phone rang without an answer, I watched a raven pecking through the half-frozen mud of the ditches. It rose, cawing, and circled to land again in the ditch. I wondered what, if anything, it had found to eat.

The answering machine kicked in. "Hi, Nate, this is Rose calling," I said. "Do you know anyone who needs a deckhand? I've got to get off the boat I'm on." I set down the receiver and squatted against the wall, out of the wind, to rest. *I guess he must be fishing*, I thought. *I guess he's gone.*

The phone rang, and I answered it. "Rose?" Nate asked. "I was just coming in when I heard the phone. Where are you, anyway? I was starting to wonder if I'd ever hear from you again."

"I'm still in Homer. I'm calling from a payphone." A flood of unreasoning happiness swept over me at the sound of his voice. I forgot how strained we'd been last time we talked and thought only of how much I'd liked him.

"Are you still fishing?"

"Yeah. Well, I've been working on a cod boat, but we brought our pots in today. The skipper's going jigging in a couple days. He's offered to keep me on, but I want to quit."

"Why?"

"Long story," I said.

"I see. I've been there," he said.

"So, do you know anyone who needs a deckhand?" I changed the subject.

"I'll hire you," he offered, "if you're willing to work for me. I'm going to be running the *Antagonizer* tender for the early season in Cordova. He's got a deal hauling fish from the Flats."

"Sure," I said. I didn't hesitate.

"Do you have enough cash to get to Cordova?" he asked.

"I think so. I can hitch to Whittier, anyway. Do you know how much it would be for the ferry?"

"No idea."

"Me neither," I said. "Well, I'll get there somehow. Guess I'll head back to the harbor now, find my skipper and tell him I'm quitting. I guess I'll be seeing you in a couple days." I said goodbye, hung up, and called the ferry terminal in Whittier. As I walked back to the waterfront to find Jay, an unexpected happiness rose in me. I didn't know whether it came from the fresh chance at fishing or from the thought of seeing Nate again.

The Salty Dawg was packed, as usual. It was dark and the air was full of cigarette smoke. A band played, though few people were listening. I edged through the crowd looking for Jay. At last I saw him alone at a table, staring ahead as if lost in thought. When he saw me coming he moved over to make space for me.

"Buy you a drink?" he said, as he always did.

"Thanks," I said.

He waved the barmaid over. I ordered a beer and paid for it when it came. Three women had gone up to the microphone. They sang a song I recognized.

"Go tell me old shipmates. I'm off on a trip, mates. And I'll see them sometime on Fiddler's Green . . ."

Jay listened closely, but when they finished he snorted in contempt. "I don't guess they know too much about the water." He gulped the last of his beer, ordered another, and lit a cigarette. "I've been talking to some people, got some tips. One guy told me about a place he put in a thousand pounds one time. We'll head out there in the morning." He winked at me, still scheming for some future, some hope. "Everybody wants to buy gray cod right now."

I started to tell him I was quitting, but another woman came up to the mike. She read a story about a boat sinking, in which the skipper had died. The Coast Guard hadn't reached him in time. Her story seemed to say that they had failed. He could have lived—he would have lived—if the rescue had come sooner.

Jay listened intently. Halfway through, he began shifting in his seat. "That ain't how it went," he said.

She finished speaking. Doug from the *Totem* shoved his way up and took the mike.

"My name's Doug," he said, too loudly. Feedback squealed. The bar fell silent. He looked up, saw the drinkers watching him, and lost his momentum in sudden stage fright. He stood for a moment unsteadily, clenching the microphone in both his hands.

"Go, Doug," someone shouted from the bar. He took a breath and began again. "My name is Doug. I wanted to say, I was there that day. I knew Tony. He was my friend. Maybe the Coast Guard could've done more to save him, but . . . well, I just wanted to say, that was some of the worst weather I ever was out in. It was bad. Boats was going down right and left, and the Coast Guard had their hands full. So don't go kicking their names around. I mean, they save our asses." He glared around the room as though daring us to disagree with him. "Just don't be kicking the Coast Guard's name around. They save our asses," he repeated, as if that could make it true. He dropped the mike and headed for the bar. A few people clapped, but already his listeners had turned away. The noise of the bar rose again.

"He's right," Jay said.

"Hey, Jay," I said. "I just got offered another job."

Jay said nothing for a moment, then, "So, are you going to take it?"

"Yeah. It's guaranteed money, for one thing. I need to make some money." I didn't add, *We never will jigging. It doesn't matter how high cod prices are, Jay, when there are no cod to catch.*

He lowered his head to the beer-sticky table and beat his forehead on it slowly, then lay with his head among the glasses, looking up at me puzzled and out of focus.

"What am I gonna do without you, Rose?" he said.

"You'll be able to find another deckhand. Jigging is easy work," I said. Jay raised his head and thumped it down again. I got up to go, leaving my drink sitting there.

"Was nice working for you," I said, and shook his hand. Turning away, I walked out of the Salty Dawg, down the now-familiar ramp into the harbor, and past the rows of fishing boats lying quietly in the chilly spring light.

I had meant to stay another night, but instead I got my backpack and started walking. The raven was still pecking away in the ditch. I said good-bye to it as I passed.

EIGHT

THE FERRY TO Cordova was late and slow. It bucked in erratic, desultory seas, the tail end of a storm from Asia. I looked out through the rain-streaked window at water furrowed with long, white swells rolling past an empty, rock-bound shore.

We docked by the cannery pier. Nate was there to meet the boat. I saw him from the dock as we pulled in, his body slumped inside his woolen shirt and the distance between us alive and warm. He looked younger and rougher than I remembered, a little lost, a little tough, leaning on his old orange pipeline truck in his scruffy beard and unwashed jeans. But he was someone waiting for me. My heart seemed to swell open, I was so happy to see him because of that. I ran off the ferry into his arms.

He drove me to the harbor to drop my pack. I left it at the top of the ramp, walked down the pier, and leaned on a piling, looking out. The water was silver, streaked with light and foam. Nate sat beside me on the rail. We talked a little about little things. He started topics and broke them off, his hands dug into the pockets of his jeans, twisting the fabric restlessly.

"So, what did you think of pot fishing?" he asked at last. "Was it what you hoped for?"

"Not quite," I said. "I was scared a lot." As I said it, I knew that it was true. I told him about that last day on the water, when my foot slipped and I thought I was going to die.

He said, "Well, that's usually how people get hurt out here." He chewed a toothpick, flipped it in the water. "You know," he said, "what scares me most, though, is the way your body can just stop working—something you've depended on all your life."

"Yeah?" I said. I hardly knew what he meant. Neither, I think, did he.

It was full dark when we reached the boat. We walked past rows of silent vessels to the *Antagonizer*, our footsteps hollow on the floating dock. He stopped before a small tender. Thirty-eight feet long, set up for buying fish from the fishermen and transporting them to the canneries. A fuel resale tank on the stern, buoys alongside, and totes ready to sling from the picking boom to transfer fish off the smaller gill-netters.

"This is it." Nate pointed at the name. He eased open the door and peered inside.

"Damon's not back yet." He turned on the light as we stepped inside the cabin, and quickly, as though it was something he'd planned to do and needed to do at once, he reached for me.

We held each other for a moment. Then, still too quickly, he slid his hands along my belt, holding me too tightly and too close. I flicked the light out, hoping things would be all right. I remember feeling, wanting it to be more, hoping and waiting, and the awkwardness and patience. I wondered if he'd been satisfied, or if either of us knew what we were missing or trying to reach, the love and rightness that can't be faked. But he did not know how to reach it, and neither did I. And even then I felt the loneliness, though it was sweet to feel his body next to mine.

I opened my eyes to a blaze of sunlight. Someone shook my arm. I rolled out of the bunk, tugging on my sweat shirt and kicking for my boots.

"It's seven," Nate said. "You want to grab a cup of coffee. We got a hell of a lot of work to do today." I stood up, dazed, and saw the window full of golden light. Outside, boats were running from the harbor mouth and men were going up and down the dock. They called to each other as they passed.

"Hey, Korey, good luck. I'll see you out there."

"Good fishing, Mike."

Behind me, Nate poured coffee from the pot.

A moan came from the other bunk. A man swung down. He looked at me, breathing hard.

"Morning." He shoved past us into the head.

Nate looked at me and raised his eyebrows.

The door swung open again. Damon backed out, buckling his jeans. He held a can of air freshener in one hand. It oozed a cloud of mist toward the floor.

"Violet fucking rose fucking potpourri," he said. "Fuck this shit." Up close, his eyes were gray, shiny, depthless, his face flushed and fleshy with alcohol. An older man, heavier than Nate.

"Coffee's ready," Nate said. "This is Rose."

"Pleased to meet you." He poured a glass of water, inspected it, and drank. "Fu-uck," he said. "We got any milk? Best cure for a hangover's milk. I feel like I've got Mongolian fucking mad-dog fever or some fucking thing. God, I drank so fucking much last night . . ." His voice trailed off.

"Have fun?" Nate asked.

"Oh, yeah," Damon said. "We started at the Anchor, went up to the Alaskan and closed it down. There was a lot of people out last night. It was crazy at the Alaskan. There was this fucking little Filipino fucker got in a fight with another motherfucker. I pulled him off and pinned him against the wall like this . . ." Damon's arm cramped shut. "If that little fucker moved I'd'a twisted his head off, but he'd had enough."

He spat and peered into the sink. His eyes met mine, seeming oddly disconnected. "Like that?" he asked. "I was in Desert Storm. We use'ta fill our canteens with sand and chuck 'em to the kids at the side of the road."

"Yeah?" Nate said. He wasn't listening. He shuffled through the papers on the table, searching until he found a list. "Mark should be here soon, he's up at the cannery," he said as he scanned it.

"Mark never gets anywhere soon." Damon said. "Hurry up and wait, that's what being a deckhand is all about. Brr—br-brrruppp," he mimicked the sound of a machine. Nate ignored him, smiling to himself, and Damon fell silent to gulp his coffee.

I poured another cup of coffee and went out on deck. A boat passed, its wake stirring the greasy calm of the harbor water, making the *Antagonizer* rock at her moorings. The sun had broken free of the horizon. It seemed to float in the effortless blue of sky. Mountains soared white above the town.

An older man was coming down the pier, limping a little as though his knees hurt him. He carried a bag of cleaning supplies that he handed to me as he stepped on board.

"I'm Mark," he said. "Hey, Rose, I've got something to show you." He beckoned me to follow down the dock.

"Mountains are beautiful, huh?" he said. "I see 'em in the morning and it makes me feel lucky. Something to wake up for. You like Robert Service? 'The freshness, the freedom, the farness—O, God! how I'm stuck on it all.' I make all my crew read Robert Service."

He pointed at the supplies in my hand. "I was hoping you'd see what you can do with these this morning. Get some of the shit off the walls if you can."

I nodded.

"Looking at the *Kanak*?" Nate came up behind us.

"Yeah," Mark said.

"I wanted to see how he mounted that circ' pump in the bilge."

He fell in step down the dock, past the rows of crabbers and the gill-net fleet. Mark stopped before one of the smaller seine boats, rigged for fishing with a skiff and purse net and pretty in the style of years before.

"This was my first boat," Mark said. "I remember running her through Shelikof Strait in weather so shitty we thought we would die." He stepped over the rail, swinging his leg stiffly from the hip, and went through the sliding door into the galley. "Two men were sitting on that bench, holding onto each other and crying. But Julie, my girl Julie, was standing beside me looking out the window like it was nothing and eating a peanut butter sandwich. I never did figure out if she was brave or dumb."

He glanced around the cabin as though he could still see them there. "That was a long time ago, now," he said. I looked, too, at the bench where the men had held each other, at the window where Julie had stood, but to my eyes the boat had no history. It was only a boat, unused now and as shabby as the men on its deck.

"When we got into Kodiak that morning, I was so happy I thought I'd cry," Mark went on. "All the way into the harbor mouth I was thinking, 'Alive! I'm still alive!' I couldn't wait to tell someone that I was *alive*. I went up to the bar, but in the end I found out I couldn't say it. I couldn't tell that story at all. I couldn't get it right."

He moved out on deck as he talked, putting his hand on the valve levers, the buoy lines, and the fish hold pump, as if they were long familiar to his touch.

"Two years after that I was hired to run the *Kanak* for herring fishing in Prince William Sound," he said. "But I woke up one morning just before the season and saw people crying on the docks. Good Friday, March 1989. The *Exxon Valdez* had gone aground."

Crude oil had dumped into the Sound, spilling from the stricken oil tanker. Eleven million gallons, as far as anyone knew.

"Guys flooded out of town, heading for the spill. We tried to stop it, just us fishermen. But we didn't have equipment, and we couldn't do much. By the time Exxon got there twelve hours later, it was too late. The wind had come up, and the slick spread out west." His eyes stopped meeting mine, as if he were looking inside at a private sorrow, though his story was a public history. I listened, and I liked him as I listened.

"Later, Exxon put us on payroll, hired us to do whatever, cleaning up. At first we worked like bastards. They told me to keep the oil from getting up Sawmill Creek and gave me this phony little boom to do it with. Every time the tide came up, there I'd be, keeping the oil back. It was a god-awful job. My crew was ready to lynch me because I wouldn't slow down. I felt like if we could just save one creek, that'd be *something*. But we lost it. And that was the end."

He looked at me again, to make sure that I understood, as if this were something I needed to know to work in this place.

"I remember the spill," I said, meeting his gaze. "I was just a kid, but I remember." It was true. I'd been twelve that spring, living in Haines and well to the east of the spill. But I remembered walking into the kitchen early that March morning and seeing my parents staring at our old black radio with tinfoil on its antenna to make the distant signal come in clear.

"Oh, bloody hell," my mother said under her breath. My father stood, carefully flexing his hands, as he always did when he was troubled, as if they hurt most of the time and hurt worse now.

"What's wrong?" I'd asked, and they told me about the spill, those millions of gallons of shadowy oil spreading in the clear green water of the Sound. I remember it sounding like the end of the world to a fisherman's kid. And maybe it was the end of a time and place.

Mark nodded when I spoke and kept on. "Nothing did much good. Most of the oil stayed out there. Hell, for most of the summer, me and all the other guys they hired were left standing by, waiting for instructions that never came. It was like Exxon didn't care whether or not the oil got cleaned up. They just wanted to spend a lot of money, because that would look good for them in court." Mark paused and shrugged, blinking. "Bastards," he said.

Nothing had changed. Another spill would come, the inevitable product of big water, greed, and oil.

"Just bastards." He spread out his hands, empty of answers, showing me there weren't even words for how fucked up things were.

"Lot of guys quit working altogether that summer," he went on. "People would go home to get away from all of it, but when they got there they'd beat their wives. Everything around us was sick and dying. You almost couldn't care anymore. It was like the whole town had broken its heart.

"We'd never seen such high wages as we got that summer, or such high prices. I made eighty thousand in four months, but in the end it was like I'd made nothing at all. The owner tried to cheat me out of some of it—too much money can make people crazy—but even if he hadn't, it wouldn't've mattered. I'd'a wasted it somehow. It was all just wrong."

He mumbled something and looked around the harbor. "See how it's changed?" he asked, but I couldn't. The scars left in the Sound and in the minds of its people had become a part of everyday life—familiar, abrasive, seemingly normal.

"The birds never came back the way they used to be. And the herring are gone. If you dig down on the beaches of the Sound, you can still find oil under the surface gravel. But we started fishing again next season. What else could we do?"

I didn't know. I told him so. But it didn't seem to matter what I said.

Nate had gone into the cabin. Now he thrust his head back out the door and broke in. "Let's check out that pump," he said. He kicked open the engine room hatches and dropped from sight.

Mark said, "He's a good guy." He sat down on the edge of the hatch and swung down carefully after him. "Let's see what you got, Nate," he said. "What we can do for a fix."

NINE

~

THE NEXT MORNING, I woke to the sound of the engine firing. Nate was up, ready to leave.

"We're heading north," he said. "The Outer Hole. The cannery called."

"Yeah?" I said. Damon was asleep.

"Can you untie?" Nate asked. "No need to wake him yet."

I slipped the lines loose and threw them in the locker, then came inside and sat down at the table.

"The eeriest thing I've ever seen was while fishing out here," he said as we left the harbor. "Mark took me out to show me the fishery. Some guy had rolled his boat in the breakers the day before. Where we were fishing we could see the wrecked hull. All day we made sets in front of it, drifting back and forth. Sometimes we could only see part of it sticking out of the water, and sometimes it was high and dry. God, it was eerie to see."

He turned the boat outside the entrance and headed north. We passed out of the inlet into a region where sea and sky stretched off together in limitless, depthless distance.

"When the tide is out, this is a maze of channels," Nate said. "Some of this water is only a few inches deep even now, with the tide at its highest. You'd never know to look at it, would you? They put up those stakes to mark it every spring, but the bars are always shifting with the tide. What I'm doing now, I'm entering our course into the GPS so I can follow it back out again." He showed me how the GPS gave a little picture of the area with the dark dash that was the *Antagonizer* moving slowly along the outlined shape of land. A dotted line marked the course we'd taken.

He tapped the next screen. "This thing is a depth sounder," he said. "That's pretty useful, especially around here. And this is the radar. If you put all the information you get from these instruments together, you can get a dim idea of what you're supposed to be doing. But even then, you have to know a lot more than you could explain. I don't yet. You know, those old fishermen back in the day, they came out here without instruments at all. They used to kind of feel their way through. But mostly, you just have to know."

The channel bent west. We passed an outcropping of granite streaked with white.

"That's Shag Rock," Nate said. "We're traveling out toward the gulf now. There's a bunch of bars between us still, but it can get crazy rough crossing in and out right here. You get the whole weight of the Pacific thrusting up into shallow water."

Damon shifted in his seat, paying no attention. He'd gotten up without saying good morning and was now deep in a Stephen King novel. The conversation lulled as the boat began to rock in gathering swells. I got out my notebook and sat at the table, writing and looking over at Nate. He bent over the wheel, a little nervous, his body bony, cramped, as though unsuited to the job at hand. He rubbed his neck as if it were permanently painful.

I think he's afraid, I wrote. I glanced up from my notebook. Looked back down and wrote, *Of course he is*.

Late in the day, we reached the Outer Hole. The sea was quiet and the winds were calm. The breakers were slight that evening on the bar. We idled through the last sunlight, passing rafts of gulls and boats anchored up, waiting for the morning fishing.

When we dropped the anchor, it fell straight down into a pearlescent stillness. But as the line came tight, I realized how I'd misjudged the scene. The ebb was picking up, and the current ran hard. The *Antagonizer* swung against her anchor line, and hung there reluctantly in place while the moving water talked under her bow, tugged at her, stretching the line out taut as a bar. The first breath of changing weather stirred the surface.

"Jesus, I hope the anchor holds," Nate said. "If it starts dragging we're fucked. We'll pile up outside before we even realize we're moving."

"Got any better ideas?" Damon said.

'No." Nate stood on deck thinking for another minute.

"Well, I'm going to get some sleep," Damon said.

We followed him into the cabin. After a moment, someone started snoring softly. I lay awake, listening to the sound of water slapping on the other side of the hull. The sheen of the surface reflected up into the cabin. I looked out through a forest of drying boots to a toolbox standing open near my face and listened to Nate's wakeful breathing in the bunk above.

In a way, I still hardly know him, I thought. I wondered what it was about him. Why did I like him so, so much, so quickly? He was a part of this place to me, exciting because it was new and because we were young. I wanted him because he seemed to belong and because I, too, began to feel a bond to this place. Was that all it was? Or was it something more? I didn't know.

Maybe he mattered to me because I mattered to him, and I both wanted and did not want that kind of love. I believed, at least, that he saw me as I really was, while to the other men who hit on me, I was just the only girl around. But I'd been so shy when I was at school; I had very little knowledge of men.

I sighed and shifted in the cramped bunk. After all, I was still so happy, lying there far past the boundaries of my former life.

Presently, the boots were joined by a pair of feet that swung down from the upper bunk, hesitated, and padded softly out the door.

"What's up?" I whispered when Nate returned.

"Just looking around, checking on things. It's going to rain."

Half an hour later someone spoke over the VHF radio. "Your anchor is dragging," he said. The rest was lost. Nate ran on deck, checked the anchor, and came back inside.

"Well, it wasn't us," he said.

"What do you want to bet everyone in the fleet just jumped out of bed at the same time?" Damon said, as he crawled back in his bunk.

There was silence for a long time. Then the anchor chain rattled, as if it had slipped. Again, Nate shot to his feet.

"We're holding okay," he reported, coming back in. "This is stupid. I'm going to get some rest."

I lay back down, but as I drifted off I could hear him tossing in the upper bunk, and I knew I could sleep but he could not. So much depended on him.

—

Next morning, the district opened for fishing at seven. We were up by five, drinking coffee and watching the fishing boats swing heavy at their lines. It was raining hard.

"If Mark was here he'd be running around looking for fish before the opener," Damon said, staring resentfully at the motionless boats. "Lazy motherfuckers aren't even up yet." He began a story about how much he and Mark had caught together once, owing to Mark's brains and Damon's own strength. But he broke off abruptly, overcome with apathy. "God, I wish I was fishing and not tendering."

Nate did not reply. He was white with exhaustion. I wondered if he'd slept at all the night before.

"You all right?" I asked.

He nodded. There was silence in the cabin for a time as we cradled our cups of coffee, watching the rain run down the windows. When I looked at Nate again he'd suddenly fallen asleep where he sat.

"It's six thirty," Damon announced a little later. Nate woke up and shook himself.

"Should we get our gear on?" I asked.

"No need yet. Look, that guy's pulling the hook."

The boat nearest us had started up. A man in rain gear, ghostly looking through the heavy rain, came out on deck to haul his anchor. He idled the boat, holding his position for moment, then swung around up to the sandbar, tossed a buoy out over his bow, and backed the boat, letting his net pay out into the water. It stretched half across the channel below our stern, lying motionless, tugged slowly in a curve by the running water.

"He's got nothing," Damon said. As he spoke, the surface broke in flying spray just where the net came nearest to the bank. "No— look at that. Must be a king he's got there."

The splashes continued, slowly abating. More fish hit the net farther out. The man and his boat drifted away. He stood on deck, his bright-orange rain gear glowing as he bent over to start hauling in his net. Half an hour later he returned. "I heard you guys were offering a bonus for fish delivered before ten o'clock," he called.

"That's true," Nate shouted back. "Got anything?"

"Just a few." He pulled up alongside us. Damon threw him a line and slid a plastic tote onto his deck. Five king salmon lay on his deck, sleek, heavy fish the color of the sea. Their wide, dead eyes watched us remotely as the man slid them one by one into the tote. Nate lowered the swinging scale to waist height and held it as I hooked it to the tote. I steadied it as it rose on the scale and swung from his boat onto ours.

"One hundred forty-three." Nate marked the weight and spilled the fish into the hold. I jumped down after them to layer them on ice. Another boat pulled up, and another.

Mark drew alongside in his gill-netter. He hung on to the rail, shouting over the sound of wind and water.

"Soon's you've cleaned these guys up, pull out of here and run south to take the closure. You should still have plenty of water to get back through the breakers."

"What?" Nate yelled.

"Go to Whitshed!" Mark shouted. His face glistened with rain. Lifting his hand, he threw his boat in gear.

Nate nodded. The last boat left, and no more came. Two gill-netters were still picking their gear. He went inside to look at the time.

"It's getting late," he said. In a moment he checked the time again, then looked in the tide table to double-check the ebb. He came on deck again, squinting to see into the distance, biting his lip.

"I hate to leave them in this swell," he said. "But if we wait much longer the tide'll be too low to cross."

Ten minutes passed. "Do I just leave?" he said aloud. His back to us, he stared at the water, clenching and unclenching his hands.

To the west, one of the other boats finished picking and ran toward us, a flash of white spray under heavy clouds. It slid along-side us. Nate glanced at his watch, then at the water, as Damon crammed the last brailer into the hold. Two fish still lay alive on deck, bleeding slowly into the scupper.

"All right, let's get the fuck out of here. I don't want to be here on the ebb," Nate said. I knew that the breakers stacked up when the tide changed and the water that had gone upriver poured back to sea. Our boat was not as seaworthy as the gill-netters for conditions like that.

We pitched the last fish down into ice and left the other boats behind. Nate ducked into the cabin to steer. I followed him. The boat was moving fast now, heading for the bar. Inside, the oil stove had gone out.

"Can you guys wipe the windows or something? Hurry. I can't see shit," Nate said. I grabbed a paper towel and started wiping.

"Damon, you sure everything is squared away on deck?"

"Yeah."

"Well, get all that shit off the table before it starts flying. It's going to get kind of lively in here. Damn it! I can't see a goddamn thing with the windows fogged up like this." Nate grabbed at the nearest window, cracking it open.

I knelt beside him, looking out where the channel gave way to surf.

"Jesus, I hope there's enough water. If there isn't, we're fucked," he said.

"Hey, you won't hear me saying we're fucked. Or if you do, you'll know we're really fucked," Damon said. "That's when we'll be finding out we've got no survival suits as the boat blows up under us."

Nate snorted in disgust. The cell phone rang. He answered it without taking his eyes from the water. "Hello? . . . Oh, yeah, we got them loaded aboard . . . yeah . . . yeah . . . we just took one more delivery . . . yeah . . . look, Mark, I have to call you back." He slammed the phone down on the console. "Jesus Christ, the fucking depth sounder shit the bed!" He stared at the instruments before him as the reading on the screen jumped up and down.

"What the fuck!" He scrubbed the glass again without effect, peering at the wall of breakers. Water crested with dirty foam surged past, spray streaming down the cabin windows. The *Antagonizer* swung sideways in the trough. As Nate tried to right us, the next crest struck us broadside on, slapping up over the wheelhouse and splashing through the open window. Again, he tried to force us back on course. A breaker shot up to our port. As it fell back it showed flashes of bare sand.

"Can you see where the channel is?" he said. "We came through there last time, but there's no water now."

"Maybe there?" I said. He wasn't listening.

"Hang tight," he said. We coasted over a crest. The water flattened out around us, until we were past the worst of the break.

"Jesus! Did you see that big one? It came through the window like a fucking fire hose!" Damon said. "I saw that wave coming, and I thought 'We're fucked!'"

Nate did not take his eyes from the water. "Shut up, Damon," he said. He hit the depth sounder again and swore as we turned west into the channel behind the bar. Sea otters drifted on their backs before us. They rolled and dived as we came too near.

"Goddamn," Nate said softly. The boat touched bottom, dragged, and kept on.

"Draggin' ass?" Damon spoke.

"Yeah," Nate answered. "But we're almost through." Ahead the channel broadened again, mudflats falling away underwater. Nate breathed a sigh as the water grew deeper. He straightened in his chair. "I need a cigarette. And Rose? We're going to need to eat."

I got up and searched the half-empty cupboards. There wasn't much. Ketchup. Potatoes. A withered onion and a bag of cereal.

"Who shops for groceries?"

"We'll load up when we get paid," Nate said. "Can you make do?"

"Yeah," I said. I put the potatoes on to boil, took a fish from the hold, and cut it up. Already, we were coming to the anchorage. Looking up, I saw the other tenders, steel-sided boats that towered over our own.

Nate edged our boat into the fleet and sent Damon out on deck to drop the hook. The potatoes had finished cooking. I added the fish and the onion, salt, and the last of the milk. When the fish turned pale, I filled a mug and handed it to Nate.

Damon came back in. The men shifted from their chairs to the table. Nate shuffled a dog-eared pack of cards.

"Play a game of Hearts?" Damon asked. Nate was already clearing space for a game, pushing back the junk that covered the table.

I got a cup of coffee and sat down. Outside, a gleam of sunshine broke through the clouds, lighting the dirty cards.

"He's shooting the moon," Damon said.

The sunlight moved across the table.

Then, "Damn, I can't stop him."

Nate laid his cards down, grinning, winning the game.

"Deal again," I said, looking at his hand.

"Better get your gear on. Fishermen'll be here soon." Damon swept the cards together. A flock of gill-netters broke over the horizon, spray blowing back along their sides like wings. They bypassed us, slowing their pace as they went through the tender anchorage.

One dropped from the race and came up to our side, skippered by a young man. Behind him, another boat pulled in. The men whipped lines around their cleats and tied them fast.

"Hey," Nate said. "How'd it go today?"

"Great." The young man grinned. I climbed onto his boat and began to pitch his fish into a tote. He had sockeyes mostly, smaller than the kings. For a moment he watched me work. Then he jumped into the hold beside me.

"This is man's work," he said. He moved me out of the way. "Let me do it."

"It's all right," I said, but he didn't answer. He pitched his fish, breathing noisily. I thought that he was drunk. I climbed out of the hold and went to help Damon on the other boat. The older man watched us, easing his back.

"That's my son." He nodded across the deck at the young man bent over, handling his catch.

"Yeah?" I said. He smiled. That was all. Damon picked up his pace when I dropped beside him, and I knew he was trying to outdo me. I followed, pitching as he did. He was stronger than I, but the weeks on the *American Eagle* had toughened my body. We finished together and swung out of the hold.

Nate made out a ticket. "Thanks again. Hope you'll bring us your fish another time."

"You bet." The old man dropped his lines and pulled away. His son finished pitching his own fish. When we cast him off, he spun along the shore, his boat half in the shallows and moving fast. As he passed out of sight we heard his voice on the radio: "Take your fish to the *Antagonizer*. They got the best price and the best-looking crew . . ."

"He's had a few shots," Damon said, already tossing a line to another boat, "if he thinks I'm good-looking."

"I guess so. Should we have done something?"

"Nah. Nothing to hurt him between here and town."

"Anyway, didn't that look like fun?" I whipped the stern line around a cleat. "I just can't believe he wasn't going aground."

"Those fucking bowpickers . . ." Damon began, looking at the boats that passed us by, fast, shallow-draft, but seaworthy gill-netters set up for hauling gear over the bow. The skipper of the next boat was having trouble getting his hatch covers off and we stood for a moment, motion arrested.

"They don't draw much, bowpickers," Nate said. "Maybe an inch or so. I've seen Mark bomb across a sandbar, nothing in his wake but mud. They get up on step, you see, get a cushion of water moving in front of them . . ."

"Crazy."

The hold was open now. We jumped in and began to pitch fish. Already Nate was tying up another boat and more began to form a line behind us. "It's a crazy fishery," Damon grunted in reply, keeping his head down, pitching fish like a machine. As soon as we finished, another boat pulled up. My arms were crusted and dripping with slime. Sweat ran down my back. I knew the men were watching me and laughing, but I didn't care.

That night we rode a wave of euphoria at the season's beginning, the smell and sound of it, the sight of the fish. That night, at least, working fast and hard with dark coming on, I wanted badly to like it.

We took fish until midnight, then ran to town and off-loaded at the cannery. It was three in the morning when we reached the harbor. By then, all of us were exhausted. There had been no time to break while taking deliveries. But we were happy.

"Ass-kickingest crew in Cordova," Damon said as we tied up the *Antagonizer*. He brought out some whiskey and passed it around. "To a hell of a season."

TEN

THE NEXT MORNING, Nate crawled from his bunk at dawn. The night before, the generator had died, as had the oil-burning stove. Now he changed the fuel filters and began siphoning diesel to clear the lines.

All day I listened to him cursing as I worked on deck. By noon he knew that the main engine was sucking fuel from the generator, causing it to starve. He began rebuilding the system so that each engine ran off a different tank. Late in the afternoon, he came on deck, dispirited, and hawked a stream of spit over the side. Full of fuel, it made a greasy rainbow on the water. "If diesel was an ice cream flavor I wouldn't even try it," he said. He'd come up only to ask me to go to the hardware store to buy some hose and hose clamps before it closed.

When I returned, he was back in the engine room. Damon was coming down the dock from the *Kanak*.

"I was talking to Bob," he said as he stepped aboard. "He's one big motherfucker. Said he might hire me for long-lining this fall."

"I thought you were going to go with Pete somebody?"

Damon paused. His grin faded. He took an angry drag off his cigarette. "I asked Pete about it this morning," he said. "That fucker. He said 'I don't know, Damon. You got to be kind of an animal to go long-lining.' I said, 'Do I look like a fucking Girl Scout?' Fuck him." Damon glared at me. "Do I look like a Girl Scout?" he demanded again. "If Bob says I can work for him . . ."

Down in the engine room, Nate laughed. Damon looked hurt. "You know, that guy's kind of a weirdo," Nate said. "They say he jerks off while he's steering."

"Yeah, but he's from here," Damon said, glaring at the hatch where Nate had disappeared.

In the early evening, Nate finished hooking up the lines. He climbed from the engine room, weary and dirty. "Let's knock off for a while. Go get a beer."

"Fuck yeah, I could use one." Damon dropped his grinder.

I laid down my tools and tried to clean my hands.

"No use trying," Nate said. "We'll get cleaned up in September." All three of us headed up the dock and along the waterfront to the Anchor bar. We had drinks already when Mark came in. He walked over, digging awkwardly into his pockets. "Thought I had my credit card. I was gonna buy you guys a drink," he said, sitting down.

"Let me get you one. I still have all my herring money," Nate offered, but Mark waved him off. "Let me see, I might still have some cash in here," he said, pulling out a fistful of crumpled bills. He beckoned the bartender over and ordered another round. Evening sunlight lay over the table. I was half-asleep from the warmth—and from working all night.

"Guess it went okay yesterday, huh?' Mark asked. Damon plunged into stories of the day before, telling how the winch had quit and he had hauled the anchor by hand, how we had been hit broadside on in the breakers so that water came through the window "like a fucking fire hose," and how we had nearly gone aground.

"Then we took fish from this crazy motherfucking kid. He'd had a few shotneys. When he left he was fucking yelling over the radio that we were the best tender anywhere, whipping shinnies up in the shallows there . . ."

Mark laughed. "Bet I know who that was. Did I ever tell you guys the story about that kid getting himself wound up on the reel?" he asked.

"No."

"He did what?"

"Was he drunk?"

"Was he all right?" I asked, forgetting I'd just seen him.

"Last season was his first with his own boat. He was over off Ester fishing with a girl. Both of 'em got drunk, and the girl passed out. Somehow or another, Roger got himself caught in the net coming in." He flung his arms up to demonstrate. "Some guys saw the boat drifting and came alongside to make sure everything was okay. They could hear him shouting, but it took 'em a while to find him and get him loose."

"Was he all right?" I asked again, half disbelieving. The story didn't make sense to me.

"Oh, he was fine. Probably didn't feel too good, though. The girl was still passed out." Mark started laughing.

Nate pushed back his chair and stood up. "Time to get back at it. We got some things to finish before tomorrow." His hand on my back, he herded us down to the boat again.

ELEVEN

MAY PASSED SWIFTLY, though the season fell into a series of fits and starts, never as much fishing time or as many fish as the men hoped for. In time, the cannery started sending us to Steamboat Slough. Mark rode with us on the first run out, his gill-netter towing behind the boat. Outside the harbor we turned west, skirting breakers on our ocean side. Nate made me stand on the bridge with him, memorizing the shapes of the channel as it unfolded.

When we dropped anchor, Mark left. Damon rigged a halibut pole over the side. I climbed onto the bridge to watch the light die, boats black on the bright water.

Nate came up after me. "Mind if I join you?" He sat down on the damp chain locker and rolled a smoke.

"I've been wondering," I said. "I've heard you guys talking about Bristol Bay. Like you might quit here and try fishing out there. Is that true?"

"Yeah," he said. "The season's shitty. We're the smallest tender out here and the least valuable. The cannery's going to lay us off. It's only a matter of time."

"And Bristol Bay?"

"It's kind of magic, or it used to be. The fish pour in there some years. You can make a hell of a lot if you can work hard enough. Mark's got a boat there, the *Shameless*, that was the first boat I ever ran." Nate looked at me. "You could probably go, too, if that's what you're after. I haven't talked to Mark about that yet, though."

"Oh." I was startled. It hadn't occurred to me that I might go. I felt so much like an outsider on the crew still, and I wasn't sure if I wanted to. "I see."

"Well, let me know," he said. We lapsed into silence. The air grew colder. Damon had long since finished setting up his gear and had gone into the cabin to wait for an unwary fish to take the hook. Somewhere beneath us, maybe a halibut was nudging it, unsure whether to bite or to keep traveling.

I was wondering that, too. Was fishing truly what I wanted to do? Or was there more, somewhere else, slipped into the past. The loveliness of the night called it out in me somehow: nostalgia, or homesickness for a place that maybe did not exist.

"Nate . . ." I said at last. "Have you ever thought of doing something else?" I wondered if it was only me, to feel this need for wandering, this nameless quest for a wilderness somewhere farther along. These daydreams, already vanishing a little in the cold gray light of reality.

He picked up my hand and held it a little too tightly.

"No . . ." he said. "Not for a while. This gets into your blood and you can't stop."

"Seems like," I said. I fell silent again. In this light, sea and sand were two-dimensional, the bars mere tracings of land on the water. In the distance, the Chugach Mountains rose into the pale fire of the sky, seeming to sever us from the world. At that moment, that place was all I'd ever wanted, whatever the consequences.

The door clicked open. Damon came out on deck. I listened as he reeled his line in slow.

"There's nowhere else on earth I'd rather be," I said.

Below us, Damon laughed softly.

"What about a Las Vegas whorehouse?" he called up.

"I wouldn't know. I've never been," I said, not wanting to let him see that he made me uncomfortable. He joked about women in an ugly way sometimes. "Have you?"

"Oh, yeah!" he said, tasting his words. "I used to work there, bodyguard. Best job I ever had. Had the most side benefits." He checked his bait and dropped it back in. I heard the door close behind him again.

Nate looked disgusted. "Trust Damon," he said, "to wreck the moment." His arm slid around me anyway.

But all my peace of mind had fallen away. I was tired of being the only woman there.

"I'm cold," I said. I stood up abruptly and went inside. That night I lay awake for a long time, trying to think what to do, whether to go on fishing or head on down the road. I'd begun to love this place, the beauty of it, the effort and event, but I did not know if I could love the men enough to belong with them. I gave up at last and fell asleep without finding the clarity I needed.

~

We stayed in the channel through the next morning. Few boats were fishing there, and we took no deliveries. I lay on deck in the sunshine, watching the *Channel Rat* drift down to the south and pick its net back up again. Another tender lay anchored near us. I saw the crew once, when they stepped out on deck to piss over the side. Other than that, the day was still, the sky a pure, unbreakable blue. The day seemed to hang suspended, so much time unused, slipping by. For long moments I thought of nothing at all, just the smell of the water; the green, salty smell of the barrier islands; the gulls crying overhead; and behind them, a wide silence. It was so lovely there; in a strange way it broke your heart because it was nothing you could hang on to. It was a place perfect in its way, unreachable.

In the early afternoon the cannery called and told us to start for

Softuk. I stayed on deck as we headed out, watching the shadows shiver in our wake. To the south, the horizon darkened to gray.

The next day the weather changed to wind and rain. Gusts slapped and whistled in the rigging. I woke to find Nate listening to the VHF, his brow creased with difficult thoughts.

"Sounds kind of snotty," he said. He turned off the radio. "It doesn't matter. The guys are fishing anyhow." He turned back to the window, watching the rain slide down it, dripping from the faulty window seal. I looked past him at a world where all the color had blotted out in grays of sky and muddy water. A few gulls still circled overhead, blown up and down in turbulent air, but others squatted on the surface of the water, letting the wind pass overhead. On the barrier island, the grass flattened as the wind passed, as if crushed by an invisible beast. *How quickly things have changed*, I thought.

Late that morning, we headed out again in an incipient gale, making for an anchorage nearer town. The prediction was for southwest winds at forty knots, with seas to fifteen feet in the gulf. The tide was ebbing hard out of the channel, and the current raced in shattered rips, cutting up the prevailing chop. After a time, Nate decided to shelter for the night rather than try the crossing on the ebb.

"We'll see what the weather looks like tomorrow," Nate said. "Maybe we'll make it on the morning tide." But once we anchored up, he got a call from the cannery telling us to stay where we were. "Guess they want us to play it safe," he said.

All the next day we kept busy taking fish, but the deliveries were small. Men were giving up, heading back to town or trying to cross the Sound despite the weather. The fish they brought were softening already. Damon said such fish were often the last of a run and when you saw them you knew the season was almost over. Another spring past, and everybody was still broke.

We took the closure at Whitshed again. In the midst of work, Mark stopped to tell us that one of the fishermen had died that day. He couldn't give details, didn't know who it was, but when he left a cloud settled over us.

Over the next hour we heard the same story from boat after boat. Someone had fallen overboard and been caught in the net, or else the net had dragged him overboard. No one was sure of much except that a man was dead. We were working too hard to talk for long, but still I was struck by the lack of surprise the other men showed. Grief, but not surprise. Someone died every summer. It had been nasty out there at the change of tide. The weather came quicker than predicted. The men we saw looked used up, only a few showing the glow that sometimes came into their faces in rough weather.

"Guess his luck must have run out," they said. That was all.

It was past midnight when we got back to the harbor. We were bone-cold and tired, but we meant to shower at the office before turning in. It was a long walk around the harbor to the other side. Damon brought up the drowning as we walked.

"Fucked up, huh?" he said, quietly for him.

"Yeah," I said.

"Did you catch that last guy telling us, he'd fished out here his whole life . . ." His voice trailed off.

Nate said, "I remember when I first realized fishing could truly kill me . . ."

"What happened?" I asked. I knew the story, but I wanted to hear it again, to hear the familiar ending. The repetition of stories reassured me, as I thought it did the others, too. It gave us a measure of control, reducing our fears by rendering them spoken. But Nate shook his head and did not continue.

"It's funny, you think of crabbers as having the dangerous jobs," I said. "Not us, so much. In town this spring, when they came back, they were talking about how surprised they were that no one had died this year."

"I'd like to go crabbing," said Damon. "Just to say I'd been. Those guys are the toughest motherfuckers around . . ."

"I'd like to see waves that big, weather that bad," Nate said. "I think it would be sort of beautiful." Then he knocked on wood.

"I would, too," I said, and knocked on wood myself.

TWELVE

⌒

THE NEXT MORNING, Nate sent me to Redden for fifty fathoms of half-inch line to lengthen the span between the picking booms. I had to wait a long time for the clerk to cut it. When I took it back to the boat, Nate told me that they'd given me three-fourths-inch line by mistake and sent me back to change it.

As I walked back along the dock, I passed two men cutting halibut on the gutting table. The planks at their feet were stained with blood. They nodded as I passed.

"You hear about the guy got drowned?"

"We did, yeah," I answered. "Never heard who it was, though."

"Skipper of the *Sea Miser.*" The speaker indicated a bowpicker tied up down the dock. "Fell overboard somehow. Know him?"

"No," I said, but as I continued down the dock the name of the boat nagged at my mind. I wondered if I'd heard of it or seen it before.

There was nobody aboard the *Antagonizer* when I returned. I lowered the picking booms and replaced the line between them, threading it through a maze of other lines, past the main boom, and through shackles on each of the picking booms. I raised them again. The line caught—I had strung it wrong. It should have gone over the main. I lowered it, restrung it, and raised it again. Something was still out of place.

A man was watching me from a seiner in the opposite slip. He walked over as I stared up at the picking booms, trying to see what was wrong.

"I see you guys over here all the time, working. What are you working at so hard?" he asked.

"All kinds of things. It's an old boat. Can you tell me, how should I have strung this line?" I asked.

He pointed out the right way to do it and stood watching for a moment before he walked away. I wished I'd said something more to him, but I was shy about talking to the older fishermen. They knew so much more than I did.

I finished stringing the line for the third time, raised the booms in place, and cleaned the deck. Shortly after, Nate came back.

"Do you know who ran the *Sea Miser*?" I asked.

"No idea. Why?"

"That was the boat that belonged to the guy who drowned."

"Oh. I see. No, I don't know that boat." Nate headed into the cabin. I followed after. He had lifted the hatches in the floor and was lying flat, trying to reach something out of sight.

"Who runs the boat across from us?" I asked.

"Bill Webber Sr. Why?" Nate finished what he was doing and sat up. "Can you go up to the grocery store and get a couple quarts of mineral oil? I think I've figured out what's wrong with the depth sounder."

"Yeah? What's that?"

"Well, you know how a depth sounder works? There's this thing called a transducer that bounces sound waves off the bottom, and that information is translated into the picture that you see on the screen. The transducer is normally mounted under the boat, through a hole cut in the hull. On this boat, though, the transducer is inside, sending its waves through the hull. Follow?"

"Yeah."

"Well, having it inside the hull, it doesn't work as well as it would do otherwise. For one thing, it tends to shift around, and when it shifts, it sometimes quits working, same as it did that time in the breakers. I'm going to try to hold it in place with Splash Zone—that's a marine epoxy. Also, a transducer doesn't work unless you've got it in some kind of liquid. Now, I've heard that mineral oil is the best for that. We've got ours in water right now, but I'm hoping that if I put it in oil it'll keep on working even though it might still shift around some."

"I see."

"So, could you get some oil?"

"Sure." I walked toward the store wishing I knew more about what was going on. *I want to fix transducers, too,* I thought. On the way down the dock, I passed the same two men. "That guy, the skipper of the *Sea Miser,* what was his name?" I asked.

"Dean Dewey," they told me. It meant nothing to me. "Oh, well," I said. "It's been bothering me. I was pretty sure I knew him from somewhere."

"Maybe you knew his son, Roger? He fishes around here."

"Yeah," I said. "I guess maybe I had met him." I kept going, thinking of the father who'd delivered to us when the season began, back when everyone still thought it would be a wonderful year. I tried to remember what he had looked like, how his voice had sounded, but his face was elusive, a shadow at the back of my mind. I'd met him once, liked him, and now he was gone. All the same, to hear his name, to know that I had seen him and worked with him, gave the fact of his death a strange weight. It was no random fishermen who had died, it was someone who had been for years an integral part of the life of this harbor.

The drowning stayed on my mind for days after that, as I knew it stayed on the minds of the others. Most of them would have known him to some degree and known that what had happened to him could just as easily have happened to them. It was a strange thought to live with, and a strange kind of sadness that spent itself

97

on a man I scarcely knew, because he was one of our own, and his death could have been ours.

—

The next day we left the harbor on the afternoon tide, stopped to pick up ice and fuel, then rode the ebb out to Egg Island to anchor there. In the morning the weather was bad with a stiff southeasterly wind and drizzling rain. Throughout the day we heard calls for assistance over the VHF radio: Somebody needed a tow. Someone else needed a part.

By the end of the day we had taken on only five thousand pounds. Late in the evening, long after we had stopped getting deliveries, we headed back to Cordova. The oil stove had broken again, and we were cold, wet, and tired.

It grew dark quickly under the heavy clouds. No bowpickers passed us now. Most of them had reached home long since. There seemed to be no one out except us, laboring slowly along the deserted coastline.

After a while, we heard another fisherman call for help over the radio. He had lost his steering and had drifted while he tried to fix it. Now he did not know where he was, and he still did not have steering. His call was answered by many different voices asking questions and offering advice, but his responses became intermittent and unclear. He seemed to be having trouble with his radio. Someone offered to look for him, but he didn't reply.

Damon had fallen asleep over the cabin table, a paperback thriller in his lap. Nate steered, chewing and spitting sunflower seeds ceaselessly.

"Can you talk to me, Rose? I'm falling asleep," he asked after a while. I finished the dishes and sat down. On the radio, the men were still talking about the lost boat.

Slowly, the lights of Cordova came into sight and grew brighter until we reached the cannery dock. A fishing boat lay tied up to it, delivering its catch under the glare of floodlights. Nate called the office and was told we could come in after it left.

He woke Damon up and sent him out on deck to start the pump. "Do we got any plastic bags?" he asked me. He took the day's records and put them in the bag I gave him. "When we dock, I want you to run these up to the office. If nobody's there you can slide them under the door."

At length, the boat finished unloading and pulled away from the dock. Nate went on top of the house to steer. Damon and I waited as long as we could before going out on the rain-swept deck to tie up. The *Antagonizer* came close in to the dock, closer, but not close enough. Nate pulled away to try again. I shook myself, stiff with weariness and cold.

The boat came in nearer. Damon and I flung tie-up lines around the creosote pilings. Nate climbed the ladder onto the dock. I followed him, holding the catch records in one hand.

The dock bustled, lurid in the glare of sodium lights. Two kids were sent down into our hold. They began pitching fish, rather slowly. I crossed the dock and climbed the outside stairs into the cannery building. It was warm in there, and dark. I stood for a moment before finding the office. It was locked, the lights out. I slipped the papers through the door.

When I returned, Nate stood beside the foreman checking his figures. The foreman was cursing about the kids. "They don't know their ass from their elbows," he said, as the crane man started to lift the first filled tote. The kids had overfilled it, and as the tote swayed back and forth on the crane hook, the top layer of salmon rose above its sides. Thirty feet above the hold, a king slid out and plummeted to the deck, missing them, but not by much.

"You want to get yourselves killed?" the foreman shouted down. "Don't fucking overfill those totes!"

"Go down there and keep an eye on those guys," Nate said quietly. "I'm not sure I trust them to separate the kings and reds. If the weights come out different from what's on the tickets, it's coming out of our pay."

I climbed down the ladder again and watched the kids. Twice I stopped them from sliding kings into a tote of reds. Once I went inside to fetch sodas for them. Fishermen were still talking on the radio. No one had found the man who'd lost his steering, and they were worried. He hadn't been on the air for a long time.

An hour later we finished delivering. Nate came back on board in a bad mood. The weights had been wrong, after all. We had brought in too much fish.

"We won't lose any of our wages for that," he said. "But some poor fishermen got screwed. I'd rather've been off the other way."

"How do you suppose it happened?"

"Either our scale is off or the one on the crane is. I triple-checked the figures while I was there."

We cast off and headed for the harbor. Another boat began delivering as we left. The radio had long gone quiet, but as we rounded the breakwater into the harbor mouth someone spoke at last. They'd found the man and he was all right. They were towing him in.

Back at the slip, Nate told us to clean the hold. We scrubbed the walls as quickly as we could, soused them down, and rinsed the deck. Then we walked across the harbor to shower.

The sky was already lightening with the dawn. "Three hours of sleep before Mark comes by?" Damon guessed.

Out of habit, we stopped to read the notices on the bulletin board outside the office.

"Hey, look," I pointed. A scrap of paper was tacked up at the side: "Thanks to everyone who helped with my dad. Gone out of town for the funeral. Back soon . . ." The name was illegible.

"Somebody's dad," Nate said. "That's too bad."

We went inside. When I stepped out of the shower I was startled by my face in the mirror. The covering of dirt and blood stripped away, it looked as white as a ghost's.

THIRTEEN

⌐⌐

THE NEXT NIGHT we came in early, before closing time. "You want to get a drink?" Nate asked when we were tied up.

I nodded. It was better than sitting on the boat.

"Fuck yeah," Damon said. We walked together up the ramp to the bar. Inside, Damon was quickly absorbed into the loudest group at the bar rail. Nate and I sat in the back. He kept his hand on my belt as if to show that I belonged to him and to keep other men from talking to me. I half understood that, and it bothered me, though I knew that almost any man there would have done the same. I wasn't something to be owned. And I'd begun to fear that he wanted more from me than I wanted to give.

He drank quickly, and I could not keep up. At closing call we thrust our way out of the crowd. It was cold outside, and the street was empty. When I tripped, he caught me and lifted me again.

"You're drunk," he said.

"I know," I said.

He followed me down to the harbor. At the boat, I stopped to catch my breath. He tried to kiss me, but I sidestepped him. He called after me, but I did not come back. Suddenly, I was very tired, sick of the tension between us, and no longer drunk. I went into the galley without meeting his eyes. When I turned again to face him, he was crying.

"Nate . . ."

"Forget it," he said. "Just forget it, okay?"

I looked away.

"I love you," he said. "And you don't love me as much as I love you." His voice was flat. "Is it because I'm a fisherman?" he asked.

I could think of nothing to say. For a moment, I believed that he did love me; but even then it seemed to me that the woman he wanted was an illusion, the kind of woman I would never be. Perfect, beautiful, devoted, and obedient, a woman from a storybook. And I thought he was right. I'd begun to care for him back north, when caring seemed touched by the magic of adventure. But I wouldn't let myself love him too much because I couldn't believe that this was what I wanted—this place, this man, this way of being. I couldn't imagine him as anything other than a fisherman, and I didn't want to commit myself to a life on the water. But right or wrong, what good were explanations? That night we both just felt lost.

I reached out and stroked his hand, trying to comfort both of us.

FOURTEEN

TWO NIGHTS LATER, Nate left for Bristol Bay. Our good-byes were strained, but I knew we both hoped to see each other again. There was still so much sweetness in him to me, as awkward as our affection was.

That afternoon I left the harbor, heading out with Damon as skipper. That afternoon he had bought a used .22, and as he steered he fired it out the window.

"Ever tried shooting skeet? . . . competition . . . I whirled around and BANG . . . motherfuckers said they couldn't believe I'd never shot skeet before . . ." I listened with half an ear while he told his stories. They were more for his benefit than mine, anyway. And I wondered what Nate was doing, where he was. The boat seemed empty without him.

We'd been late leaving town. The men were fishing by the time we reached Egg Island. Our VHF was on, its volume low. A murmur of voices mingled with Damon's tales.

"*Bizzy Ditch, Bizzy Ditch.* Are you there, Sue? Let's go up a couple." A burst of static. "Can I get a time check?" someone asked. More static flared, then, "Aah, this is the *Miss Emily* tendering for Norquest. We're off Grass Island Can in one hundred feet of water.

We've got ice and fuel. Stop on by if you need anything." Another man's voice, "Hey there, *Miss Emily*, aah, what's Norquest paying, do you know?"

The *Miss Emily* named his price: Ninety cents, lower than I'd heard yet.

Silence for a moment, then, "Did you guys hear that? Norquest just came out with ninety cents."

Damon's mouth dropped open. "Norquest is fucking breaking the contract?"

"Oh, Christ." I cranked up the volume. The radio screeched. Someone shouted.

"NORQUEST IS BREAKING THE CONTRACT, GUYS!" A clatter of voices. "What are they paying?' "What are the other canneries paying, do you know?" "Those MOTHERFUCKERS." "I've just got to say, DON'T *FUCKING* GIVE THOSE *FUCK*ERS A FISH."

Damon and I stared at each other. Early in the season the fishermen and canneries had struck a deal guaranteeing a minimum price per pound. Now that they had skimmed the most lucrative part of the season, Norquest had broken the contract.

"If Norquest breaks now, all the canneries will follow," Damon said. "They'll have to."

"Those fuckers," someone said again. "Those fuckers." An inarticulate groan.

The phone rang. It was our boss at the Copper River Seafoods office. No one knew how to react yet, he said, but for the time we were still offering contract price. Damon grabbed the mike and sent that news out on the VHF. But in the next hour, all the other companies dropped. The radio choked up with voices.

A man cut through the static. "Listen, guys, let's just all make sure we deliver to Copper River tenders only." Others followed, repeating him. It must have seemed a symbolic act at least, though most of them could not go through with it. Too many owed money to the other canneries.

"We're going to get fucking trampled," Damon muttered, all the same. We were the only Copper River tender in the area.

By dusk, boats lay packed up alongside us, waiting for a chance to sell. I knew it couldn't be long before we'd have to stop taking deliveries. But hours slid by without word from the office, and in the meantime we took fish as quickly as we could. There was a desperation in the work I hadn't known before, born out of the set, grim faces of the men. Since the season began, they had relied on their contract. It had been almost a promise that they would stay solvent one more year, and its failure meant not all of them would make it. I was a stranger here—my ties were shallow, I could leave. But to them, the price of fish was more than money. It was the debt paid for their blood and sweat and the means to hang on for another season.

After a while, Mark came aboard to use our phone. He had to reach the office, he said. I handed it to him, not meeting his eyes. "Keep buying?" Damon shouted.

"Keep buying," he said. I kept making out fish tickets in the galley, struggling to hear the numbers Damon called out over the roar of engines and the screech and whine of the VHF.

Mark paced as he talked, his free hand clamped over his other ear. In a moment, he stopped to ask what we had on board. I scrambled through the stacks of paper for the tally. When I told him, he flinched.

The crowd of boats around us swelled, and the water grew chaotic with competing wakes. The *Antagonizer* pitched back and forth. I grew sick peering at the dancing figures.

"We've GOT to stop buying!" Mark insisted into the phone. He shouted to Damon, "Tell them we're not buying any more!"

"What about the guys who've been waiting?"

"All right. Whatever." Mark was back talking to the cannery. In a moment he hung up. "Start for town," he said to Damon. "We can't take any more."

I ran on deck to haul the anchor. Another gill-netter was pulling up to us. I waved him off. "We're not buying," I called.

He edged in closer. "I've just got a few. Can't throw them back, won't deliver to anybody else. What in hell am I supposed to do with them?"

Mark leaned out the wheelhouse window. "Either we quit, or the company goes under. We're not going to break the contract. We've got to see what happens . . ." He told the man to keep the fish for his own use. As he spoke, the anger on the other man's face faded into weary disappointment. He let go of our rail and drifted silently down channel.

Mark closed the window and dialed the office again.

That night, the trip back took an eternity. We bucked the tide, heavily loaded, and the ebb cut our speed to three knots. I lay in my bunk after Mark left, waking now and then to see Damon hunched over the wheel in the half light, chewing sunflower seeds. Our eyes met once. He was mumbling curses at the stupidity of the company that had told him to cross at night on a falling tide. He did not stop to speak to me.

Two other boats lay in line before us. It was four in the morning before we reached the dock. At that hour, the other fishermen were asleep, but the cannery workers would be up for hours, maybe days yet, dealing with the fish. In the sodium glare of the dock lights, the faces of the dock crew were all but stripped of humanity. The Filipina woman checking weights swayed on her feet with exhaustion. Her head dipped as though she were falling, and she shivered violently. I stood beside her, checking the figures, while the crane swung brailers up and down. It seemed to keep time to the sound of the shouting men and the squeal of forklifts moving ice and fish, the pounding human blood and tired muscle.

Mark came across the dock to me. "You keeping track?" he

asked me quietly. His face, too, sagged with weariness. His shoulders slumped inside his rain gear.

"Yeah."

"Listen," he said. "I heard from Nate. They had a million-fish opener in the Bay yesterday. I need Damon here to run the boat for a few more days—the fishermen may strike, but we don't know that for sure—but I think I'm gonna send you out there now. That way Nate can at least get his net in the water. I'll send him a guy as soon as I can."

"Okay." I shrugged. I was going to Bristol Bay. The woman beside me looked at me and said, "Good-bye," or maybe, "Good luck."

Damon stepped out of the cannery door, carrying coffee and a slice of cold pizza. He handed it to me. "Breakfast," he said. I held it in my teeth as I climbed down to the boat, and the taste was unfamiliar, mixed with the smell of salt and blood.

Packing took only a moment. In the cabin, I shoved clothes into my pack, put rain gear and boots in a garbage bag, wished briefly that I had another book. Then, back outside, up the ladder to the dock. "I'm ready," I said.

Mark looked down. "Good," he said. "You'll like the Bay. When the fish are coming in and your net goes out—there's no other feeling like it in the world."

I smiled at him, and for a moment, the work seemed to light up once more with the magic of something far away.

FIFTEEN

THE NEXT DAY, I got a seat on a flight to King Salmon. It was loaded with Hispanic men and tired-looking Asian women going out to work in the canneries and with muscular, sullen, white teenagers who looked like fishing crew. As we took off, they seemed to breathe a collective sigh of weariness and hope.

Heading west, the land fell into low-lying tundra scored by vast, brown rivers. Lakes dotted what land remained so that in places it seemed not so much solid earth as a half-liquid frame for still more water. There was no sign of human habitation. Though thousands had fished the Bay in its heyday, few had stayed past the end of the season. Descending through the sky, I saw only a handful of buildings, a wind sock, and the lone runway below me.

Nate met me when I got off the plane.

"I'm glad you got here. Mark's found another deckhand, a guy named Rob, but he won't be here before tomorrow evening."

"Yeah?" I said. He bent and kissed me. "I'm glad you came," he said at last.

"I am, too." I squeezed his arm. I was happy to see him all the same. I'd missed him even more than I expected.

They were bringing the luggage in. I found my pack in a pile at the edge of the tarmac. He took it from me and slung it over his shoulder.

"Truck's across the street. I'd buy you a drink before we go, but we're in a hurry. There's an opener at six a.m. in the Egegik River. It'll take us a while to get there, and the boat isn't even in the water yet."

"Tomorrow morning, huh?"

"Yeah. I wish Rob was going to be here. You're so green. I can help you with some of the stuff on deck, but for the rest you'll have to do the best you can." Pacing ahead, he looked tired and harassed.

The road was dusty despite recent rain. Birds sang in the roadside brush, but the place had a feeling of immense space and a remoteness untouched by man.

"Price for reds is low this spring," Nate said. "Fifty cents."

I shrugged.

"Might rise, though, later in the season."

"Hope so," I said. But I had already stopped worrying about that. Someone older than I might have understood that the price of Bristol Bay fish could keep on falling, caught in a downward spiral driven by the cheap, disastrous flood of fish being farmed and harvested worldwide. But as I rode into Naknek in Nate's beat-up truck, I was just happy. Pot-fishing had been a bust for me. I'd made only a few hundred working on the tender. But I thought I might find a fortune in the Bay, and even if I didn't, I didn't care much. I believed that I'd found a wilderness that satisfied my heart.

We turned off where a slough cut inland from the river. A boatyard lay along it, a handful of fishing boats, a row of sheds, and a sign that said "Ralph's Yacht Club."

"That's ours," Nate said. He pointed at a boat on the far side of the yard. Weeds grew up between the blocks and a row of old tires hung from nylon line along its gunwhales. A window lay beside it, broken out.

I stopped. "What are those for?" I asked at last, nodding at the tires. I heard the dismay in my voice.

"They're to protect her sides. Bristol Bay is kind of a combat fishery. Boats crash into each other all the time. You'll understand when you see it happening." Nate's voice was hurt. He'd wanted me to like her.

"The *Shameless* is mine," he said. "She was the first boat I ever ran. Mark thinks he owns her, but he's wrong."

I forced a smile. When I stepped on deck, it buckled underfoot. Dried herring roe plastered the rails. "The smell will die down soon," Nate said behind me. "I found what was left of a herring earlier."

The cabin door had partly rotted away. Nate opened it carefully. Inside, the air was close with age and winter mold. He put his hand on mine and pointed at the bunks.

"Two people could fit in one of those," he said. "They're nice, aren't they?"

I nodded, still not meeting his eyes.

He said, "Don't worry, Rose. She's a sweet boat."

I didn't answer. We went outside again. Herring gear had to be dragged off the deck into Mark's locker and salmon nets loaded on board in their place. The bags were frayed; some tore as we grabbed them.

"The nets inside aren't worth much, either," Nate said. "They're full of holes. Mark ought to get new ones, but they're bloody expensive. He says he'll do it when Exxon pays our claim. Whenever that is." He shrugged and swung the net bag up on deck into the growing pile.

Already, the day was failing fast. The tide was rising and soon Ralph would come to haul the boat into the water. After loading the nets, we went through the locker gathering odd bits of gear: spare pieces of line; a buoy hook; survival suits musty with age, to be checked for damage; piles of the heavy brailer bags that lined the compartments of the hold.

"And more tools," Nate said. "We can't forget those." A wrench set. Life rings. We threw these things from the ground onto the boat. As we worked, the light changed from ordinary day to the queer, pale gleam of a northern summer night. It would not be wholly dark here for weeks to come.

Just after midnight, Ralph came with his tractor. He backed the lift under the *Shameless*, knocked the blocks out from under her, and dragged her down to the riverbank. She seemed to wake under our feet as she took to the water, a live thing still, despite her shabbiness. Beside me, Nate stood at the wheel, steering out into the river and smiling as he got the feel of his boat again.

The tide was turning, and the shore-bound setnetters had their nets out, the inshore end moored at the beach, the other anchored in the river. They worked from skiffs, going down their gear, picking fish out one by one. Nate scanned them as we passed.

"That guy's got a nice haul." He pointed at a man whose net lay just below a sandbar. Its pale corks bobbed, pulled down by the weight of fish. "See, he's getting the fish ebbing off that bar." His voice quickened. "That'll be us in a few hours." I stepped closer. He slipped his arm around my waist.

The current was strong, carrying us swiftly downriver, past the canneries and the little beach cabins where the setnetters lived, into the widening waters of Bristol Bay. As soon as we left the river mouth it faded behind us into the flat line of the coast. There were no landmarks, no trees, buildings, mountains. Nothing broke the lovely, empty sweep of sky and sea but a few fishing boats, the riding lights at their mastheads showing like stars.

"How long is the run to Egegik?" I asked at last.

"Six hours," Nate said. "I'll have you take a watch." His excitement faded, he looked tired. I wondered if he'd slept at all since he reached the Bay.

"All right," I said. I climbed into his chair.

"There's not too much to worry about here," he said. "Nothing to hit, a straight course and a calm night. Just follow the track line on the GPS, and keep an eye on the gauges." He watched for a moment, then said, "You'll do okay. See that star on the horizon?

Use that as a visual. Wake me up if anything changes or if you get off course. Wake me up in half an hour anyway." He kicked off his boots and crawled into his bunk.

I gripped the wheel, peering out. But I was too tired to be afraid for long. In half an hour I was holding a straight course. I called Nate softly. He shot upright, cracking his head on the sill. "What?" he said. "What's wrong?"

"You told me to wake you in half an hour."

"Oh. Oh, yeah."

"Sorry I startled you."

"That's okay," he said. "There's no good way to wake me." He looked at the screen. "Looks like you're doing all right. Your turn to hit the rack now."

I got in my bunk. He let me sleep for half an hour, then we changed places. That night we were both too tired to steer for long.

"I'm getting weak in my old age," Nate said, as he woke me for the third time. "We shouldn't be this worn out—we haven't lost that much sleep yet."

I grunted in reply, unwilling to agree. The night seemed neverending. Turn by turn we steered, and the hands crept round the clock further and later. But the hands of the clock seemed to bear no relation to us. We were anywhere and nowhere, two people adrift on a coast that was indifferent to our efforts.

For all that, we reached Egegik when the clock indicated, justifying its steady revolution. Nate ran the boat up inside the river. We dropped the anchor. It was an hour before Egegik opened for fishing that period. The districts in Bristol Bay opened irregularly and at short notice to manage for high-volume, swiftly changing numbers of incoming fish. Knowing this, I hoped to sleep, even for an hour. Instead, Nate made me memorize my job.

"Normally you could learn this as you go from the other deckhands. But right now, you're all I've got," he said. "You have to know." I couldn't argue. In any case, it was now near morning, and our weariness lessened with the returning day. I listened as he tried to show me how I would set the net and then stand by as he ran its length to drive in fish.

"Now," he pushed away his notes. "The last thing is, Rose, if you fall overboard, you will probably drown. The currents are so strong around here, you'll be swept away before I could reach you. And this river water is half silt. It would gather in your clothes and pull you down."

I nodded. He shook his head, shrugged his young shoulders as if to clear whatever bad luck might come of such talk, and sent me out on deck to haul the anchor. It was cold outside. A rim of violent orange circled the sky under gathering clouds. I knelt by the winch, watching as the anchor rattled up past the broken safety.

Inside, I gulped another cup of coffee as Nate ran the boat upriver, looking for a place to set.

"It was here two springs ago, I saw Mark set," he said.

To me, it all looked the same—blank river bluffs half-hidden in shadow against the ever-moving muddy waters.

A moment later he headed outside and took the wheel from the bridge. I followed him. We saw the orange flash of a buoy against the water.

"Someone's jumping the gun," Nate said.

Another appeared, and another. "Let 'er rip," he cried. I flung the buoy and he gunned the throttle, running wide open across the channel. The net flew out over the stern, dragged by its weight in the water. As the last shackle ran out, the towline rose up taut, dragging the net behind the moving boat. Nate cut the throttle and shouted, "Buoy it."

I leaped to grab the towline overhead, snapped on the buoy, and disconnected the line. "Okay!" I shouted.

Nate swung the boat. He ran the length of our net, shouting as fish struck the web. Sections of the corkline disappeared, pulled under by the weight of hanging bodies.

"All right," Nate glanced at me. "Now grab that buoy and get the towline on."

I caught it as we pulled alongside.

"Okay," I yelled again.

Nate gunned the throttle. As the line came taut, he towed the net in a hook so that the fish, following it as they followed the myriad currents and obstructions of the river bottom, would find their passage blocked and strike the web.

"Buoy," he called. I snapped the buoy on again and freed the towline. Twice more he ran the length of the net, then killed the throttle and came down on deck.

"Let's pick it up. I think we've got whatever's here. We'll head outside and look for traveling fish."

He snapped the towline to the reel and started the hydraulics. As the reel spooled, the net came in, wrapping around it. A sockeye tumbled over the rail. Nate stopped the reel to pick it from the net. His fingers slid up through the web to free its gills. It fell on deck. I grabbed the next. It was harder than it looked. I fumbled at the tangling mesh.

"You'll get the hang of it." He ducked under the net, facing me. I brought the net in another foot. Three more salmon swung over the stern.

As we worked, the boat drifted with the current. I saw a mooring buoy as we passed, a heavy thing anchored to the river bottom. It was pulled half-below the surface by the force of the current, and the water pouring over it had an ugly look. Farther down, the tenders lay at anchor. Each displayed the banner of the company it bought for: Snopac, New West, Trident. They were massive boats, eighty feet or more, able to cope with a tremendous volume of fish. Most worked as crabbers in the winter months and were built to withstand a winter ocean, flush decked and all but windowless.

Past the tenders, the fleet clustered, each boat intent on its own gear. As we drew near the river mouth, Nate pointed over my shoulder.

"Can you see that?" he said. Far off, a boat lay in the surf just outside the bar.

"I can't figure out what those guys are doing. Hang on." He ducked under the net and went inside. "Hey, there's a boat drifting off the bar. Anybody know anything about that?" I heard his voice on the VHF.

No one came back to him.

"Guys're out on deck, picking fish," he said when he came back on deck. "Can't be bothered to answer the call. We're gonna round haul this and head over there."

"Round haul?"

"Yeah," Nate said. "It's quicker. I'll show you how. We'll drag the net by hand and pile it on deck. We can get the fish out later." He grabbed the corkline as he spoke, pulling it hand over hand. Half the net still lay in the water, seventy fathoms long and heavy with fish. I seized the leadline beside him and pulled as he did.

As the last of the web came over the rail, he turned and ran for the steering wheel. Ahead, the other vessel drifted in shallows, half-obscured by breaking surf.

As we drew near, two men came out on deck.

"Get that heavy line out of the locker behind me," Nate shouted. I dragged it out and over to him. He threw a knot in it and lashed the end to the cleat on our stern. "Get ready to throw that," he said, and took control of the *Shameless* again, edging in toward the other vessel. The deckhand balanced on its bow, waiting to catch the line. Behind him, another man clung to the wheelhouse, watching.

"Throw it like you've got a pair," Nate shouted. I flung the line, which uncoiled as it flew. It landed short. I dragged it back and tried once more. The skipper grasped it and held fast. He whipped it around a cleat on the bow.

"Got it," he shouted. Nate ran back to the wheel and took control of the boat again. He gunned the throttle and the line came tight. The boats moved sharply out together, heading for deep water. The deck bucked against us, swooping up to slam us to the floor and falling away as we pitched over a crest. But we had gone through the worst of the break now, and the water grew calmer as it grew deep.

Nate's eyes met mine from the bridge. He pointed at the other boat.

"Keep an eye on the towline," he mouthed. I braced myself against the cabin and watched it arc loose and snap tight again as the boat surfed down the swells behind us. On the far boat, the man raised his hand, giving a thumbs up. I also held my thumb up, though suddenly it seemed absurd.

On the bridge above, Nate cut the throttle.

"Okay?" he yelled. The man nodded.

"Where am I taking you?"

"The *Defiance*." He pointed upriver at the tender anchorage. Nate nodded and gunned the boat again. I climbed up the ladder to stand by him.

"Everything okay?" he asked. I nodded. He freed an arm to grasp my shoulders.

"Can you get that net back on the reel?" It lay awash on the stern, a pile of web and dying fish. I squatted on deck to untangle it. We were inside the river now, dragging against the current and the ebbing tide.

The opener was over, and boats poured by, heading for the tenders. One by one they passed us, new aluminum dual pickers with twin jets, fat Modutechs, and wooden boats that had fished the Bay since before I was born. *Butterfly, Gramma Doll, Little Dominick*. So many boats, all caught up in a fever of fishing, running with us, tired, excited. Most were deep loaded. We were not.

When we reached the *Defiance*, Nate maneuvered the other vessel up to its side. The tender crew threw a line, and I cast off. We drifted alongside and caught the gunwhale.

"Hey, thanks again," the skipper said. Both men looked down. He reached into his pocket and tried to hand across a wad of crushed and swollen bills.

Nate backed away, shaking his head. The skipper shrugged and thrust the bills back inside his pocket.

"You know, I called my buddies when I first broke down," he said. "Before I killed my batteries. Said I was drifting into trouble. Those bastards—they wouldn't help me. They said they were busy catching fish. I could've drowned for all they cared. Bastards."

Nate nodded. The tenderman leaned down over the rail. "You guys gonna deliver?" he asked Nate. "Could you go around to the port side? This crane don't work."

"Yeah, sure," Nate said. He let go of the other boat. "So long," he said. "Hope you get her figured out."

The skipper nodded. We pulled away and around the tender's stern. Its steel sides cut us off from the other boat as if it had never been.

"Poor bastards," Nate said. "But that guy was an idiot. First thing he should've done when he lost power was to drop the hook. And for fuck sake, don't keep trying to start a dead engine 'til you kill your batteries . . ." He stopped and, with a visible effort not to bitch, said, "Guess it could happen to anybody."

He ducked indoors and came back out with his fishing license. "Might as well deliver what we got."

"How'd you do?" One of the tender deckhands grinned down at us.

"'Bout a thousand pounds." Nate swung over the rail and up on deck. The tenderman lowered the crane hook. I grabbed it and clipped it to the straps of the first brailer. It swayed upward, out of the hold. Five hundred pounds of salmon.

"Keep out from under," Nate called to warn me. I backed away. A few fish slipped out of the brailer and fell back into the blood and water that filled the hold. When the deck was clear, I jumped in and grabbed them. They were flattened by the weight of others, their sides imprinted with the coarse weave of the brailer bag.

The second bag went up. The men cast us off, and the current swept us quickly astern. Nate turned and headed upriver, steering from the bridge. I stood beside him, watching the tenders work as we passed, the boats crowding alongside them. Overhead the sky was silver, streaked with light and rain.

"You know," Nate said quietly. "That guy's partners could've killed him. And you know what else? I was so, so disappointed when he offered me cash. I wanted it to be different . . ." His words trailed off.

"But a beer," he said. "If they'd offered me beer . . . you could see they were drinking? God, I could go for a beer."

SIXTEEN

⸺

THE NEXT MORNING I was the first to wake. I crawled out of my
bunk and stood barefoot in the cold cabin, looking out at the
still-darkened river. We had anchored far upstream, above the village
of Egegik. The water was smooth but for the current, and what sky
I could see was heavily overcast. Steep grassy bluffs lined the river,
cutting off the world. I put on the coffeepot, enough for three.

The night before, we'd tried to anchor in the river mouth, but
the wind had picked up. It grew too rough to sleep. Near midnight,
Nate decided to look for calmer water. We idled upriver through
crowds of boats, each one silent, facing the current. It was strange
to see them in this desolate place, a floating city as transient and
shabby as a refugee camp. And maybe that was what it was—a camp
of misfits, refugees from the outer world.

Rob arrived as we were going back inside. He'd come in late
and bummed a ride from the village in someone's skiff. I had met
him back in Cordova and remembered him for the fact that his
front teeth were missing, a sight that was jarring against his clean-
cut face. A fight, I'd thought when I first saw him at the bar one
night.

"No. Meth," Damon said. Rob came up behind us then, and

Damon had swung around on his seat and said, "Hey, bitch lips, what's up?"

"What'd you say?" Rob said, startled.

"Did I stutter?" Damon stared him down. Rob looked away, pretending not to hear, and down the bar someone said, "Pussy." A nameless shiver passed lightly through the bar, as the men looked to see if they would fight. I turned away. I thought of that exchange that night, and the thought had kept me lying awake. I was glad when the day began.

"Coffee's up," I said now. Nate swung to his feet. "Want me to pull the anchor?"

"I'll get it," Rob said from his bunk. "You made the coffee." He took his cup out on deck. We slipped downriver, heading for the sea. The wind had strengthened in the night. It came from the west, tearing the surface and churning it into a steep, driven chop.

Near the river mouth we started seeing fish and idled back to wait for the opener. A crowd of other boats surrounded us, their wakes cutting up the water. Overhead, silver clouds were closing in.

I stared at them, nervous. Down on deck, Rob began to vomit.

"Hope that weather doesn't come any closer," Nate said. He looked back at the deck. "Are we ready?"

"Yeah," I said. The night before, we'd pulled the net off the reel and stacked it for a faster set. I climbed down and waited, buoy in hand. Rob wiped his mouth and straightened, watching.

"Let 'er rip!" Nate called.

I hurled the buoy overboard and watched the net whip out over the stern, uncoiling from the top of the stack. Halfway through, a broken cork snagged on the web. The net caught short as it went out, and the stack tumbled uncontrollably toward the stern.

"Hold it!" Rob yelled.

Nate cut the throttle. We struggled to drag back the mass of web, unhooked the cork, and started setting out again, but the stack was wrecked and the net caught twice more. As the last of it went out over the rail, Rob slumped to the deck, puking into the scupper until even the bile was gone, and he retched dryly, help-lessly, at the sea.

"Hey, man, you going to be okay?" I asked. I crouched over him. I was nauseous too, but nothing like that. "Can I get you something?"

"I'll be fine," he said.

Nate looked back at us. "Hey, Rob! You can lie down if you want," he called. "I'll get you up when I need you."

Rob nodded and stumbled into the cabin. In a moment, his head appeared through the door again. He lay across the threshold, heaving spasmodically. I handed him a bucket and a can of pop. He muttered thanks.

"Let me know if you need help," he said, though he looked too sick to stand.

Nate came on deck to help me bring in the net so that Rob could stay in his bunk. The sun broke out through strange pearlescent clouds, and the waves that towered over our stern were shot through with light. I could see the net inside the water and the fish in it. As each crest shattered against the boat, a welter of spray flew across the deck.

Fragmented, the mist burned away. The sky turned clear and the breeze sprang higher, cold and fresh, washed clean by miles of ocean water.

I leaned back, looking at Nate and at the fish that hung inside the sea. My face burned with salt as a wave passed. He caught my eye looking over the net.

"Rose . . ." he said, "love me, do." In a voice still almost too young, he sang, "I'll always love you." The tune faltered. He picked another.

The door swung open. Rob stumbled out to retch again.

"You guys need help?" he said when he caught his breath.

"No," Nate said. "You just rest."

Troubled, I watched him vanish into the cabin, wondering if he would be all right. Nate bit his lip.

"I'd heard that Rob got seasick a lot," he said. "But he's been fishing for a while. He shouldn't be this sick. I hope to hell there's nothing else wrong with him."

The wind stayed strong throughout the afternoon. It drove the fish in from the ocean, and we did well. After delivering, we anchored in calm water near Coffee Point. Nate and I went on deck to mend the net. We talked of Rob, wondering when he would recover, but we'd finished the work before he left his bunk.

He edged past us in the cabin and out on deck. A moment later he thrust his head inside.

"Say, Nate?" he said. "It's not good to vomit blood, right?"

Nate looked at me. I shook my head.

"No, Rob, that's not good," he said. "You doing that?"

"Yeah." Rob disappeared again. The sound of his retching filled the cabin. When it stopped, he came inside and sat down at the table with us. "Sorry about this, man," he said. "Guess I'm not much help to you."

"That's not the problem," Nate said. "What worries me, Rob, is wondering if there's something bad wrong with you. You shouldn't be this sick."

"I think it's an ulcer. On a long-lining trip once, shitty weather, I threw up for six days straight. Lost twenty-five pounds in a week. My stomach's been kind of bad ever since."

"A bleeding ulcer . . . I don't know much about medicine, but I'm pretty sure that's a bad thing, all right," I said.

"Do you think you're gonna get better?" Nate asked.

"Dunno," Rob said.

"I guess what I'm saying is, do you need to see a doctor? I can get you on a plane out of here if you need to go. It's your call."

Rob sat for a long time, thinking. Then he said, "I hate to do it, but I have to go."

He was gone within the hour. Nate called Mark after he left to tell him what had happened. They argued over the phone for a long time. When Nate hung up he looked angry, almost helpless.

"Mark just bitched me out for letting him go," he said. "Mark didn't know how sick the guy was, though. I told him, 'He was puking his guts out,' and he said, 'All fishermen puke their guts out.'"

"Harsh."

Nate shrugged. "The hell of it is, I can see where he's coming from. He spent a thousand bucks to get Rob here, and the guy quit after one opener."

"What's going to happen now?"

"He's going to try to send Damon and Travis up here tomorrow afternoon. Damon doesn't want to come, but Mark's trying to talk him into it. In the meantime, it's you and me, baby."

"I like it this way," I said.

He looked at me. "You're doing good. But if the fish start to pour in, as I hope they will, everything's going to depend on speed. We'll be fishing on the line. That can get ugly. One deckhand isn't enough for that kind of work." Nate got up. "Anyhow, we'd better hit the rack."

He crawled into the bunk without undressing. I heard the rhythm of his breathing change. I stood to follow. He was so tired still, I thought. I wondered if there was rest to come or if it would always be like this. I slipped into the bunk and held him close, but I fell asleep almost before I knew I was lying down.

SEVENTEEN

DAMON ARRIVED AS we mended gear in the afternoon of the following day. Travis, he said, would be along that night. They had separated in the Anchorage airport when Damon got a seat and Travis did not.

Damon had started chewing snoose since I saw him last. He spat copiously when he finished his speech, wedged himself along the table, and began making a spit can. He hacked the lid off an empty pop can pulled from his pocket and packed in a layer of paper toweling to absorb the juice.

"Back in the FUCKing Bay," he said. "Goddamn. I wouldn't've come except Mark was desperate. He said, 'I need you, Damon. You're a fucking animal.'" Damon finished his can and christened it with the wad of tobacco he'd been chewing. His broad shoulders and surge of noisy talk filled the cabin to overflowing. "Now I've got a can and tobacco, I can sit all day. We were working so FUCKing hard back in Cordova. The fishermen went out on strike. We fucking stayed in the harbor and got all our shit ready to fucking go seining. I'd about had enough of that tendering crap, anyway . . ."

"What happened with the strike?" I asked. "Are they going to get the contract price again?" I'd worried about the men I'd begun to know.

"Nah. Bunch of fuckers don't know what they're doing. They hung around town and argued for a while, and then they all went fishing again. Big fucking deal." He waved his arm to say that was all there was. It had happened before. It would happen again.

I stared at him, doubtful, but he was telling the truth. The price of fish in Cordova stayed below contract minimum for the rest of the season, and there was nothing the fishermen could do. After a time, they even voted to release Copper River Seafoods from their contract since under the circumstances the company could not honor it and remain solvent, but the gesture was meaningless because, by then, Copper River, too, was paying below contract price.

Travis arrived later that night. We heard a skiff idle alongside us, bumping the tires, and hurried out on deck to say hello. In the bottom of the skiff, Travis sat on his gear, a faded hoodie pulled over his head. He tossed his duffel up on deck and climbed aboard with quick, animal energy.

"Hi, guys," he said. And then, "Back in the fucking Bay," as Damon had done. But he was so young that in his mouth the words were ludicrous. He grinned until his eyes met mine. Then the grin faded into startled anger and an expression that I couldn't read, in some lost territory between wistfulness and contempt.

"She works on this boat?" he said, incredulous.

"Yeah," Damon said. He shrugged.

"Huh." Travis turned back to the men.

We never were introduced. I stood, the smile fading from my face, hoping in my heart that I misunderstood.

∼

The next morning Nate got up two hours before the opener to look for fish. It was a gray, misty morning with few fish showing. We listened to the slow, early-morning chatter of fishermen on the radio. Nobody was seeing much. "Guess they cleaned up the fish yesterday," Nate said, his mouth tight with the disappointment he tried to hide.

At ten to six, I dragged my rain gear on and went on deck. Damon and Travis crowded by the cabin door, smoking cigarettes limp with spray. We got the net ready and cleared the deck, then stood waiting. I watched a dark, quick bird dart past the boat. A jaeger, I thought. I wasn't sure.

"Let 'er rip," Nate called. I chucked the buoy over. The bird turned back and drifted past as we set out. Gulls gathered overhead, screaming and fighting over scraps that washed from the outgoing net. As they crowded up, the darker bird dived through the flock. The gulls whirled from its path.

"Do you know what kind of bird that is?" I asked Damon. He shook his head.

Travis said, "It's a black gull." He shrugged, contemptuous.

"No, it isn't, though. I wish I had a bird book."

"Look, there's something you don't understand," Travis told me. "This is just a job. We work until we go home. I don't give a fuck about the local birds."

"Well, I do," I said. I didn't understand how Travis could fish without caring about this place. It must seem like a lousy job to him, I thought, with just the dream of money and the endless hours. He would be one of those who quit after a season or two.

"If this was the old days, we could take Mark's shotgun and blow a few of them away between sets," Damon suggested. "I'd care about them then. They'd be fucking entertainment central."

Nate ran the *Shameless* along the net as we spoke. Our eyes followed the corkline, waiting for fish to hit. Nothing.

"Pick it up," he yelled. Damon hooked the buoy, clipped it to the reel. I ran the hydros. The guys watched me as I held the lever, watching the net spool empty on the turning reel.

"That's a big job for a little girl," Travis said. He let his fingers trail through the mesh as it drifted past. Abruptly, he shouted and threw himself sideways, grabbing the web as if his hands were caught. I slammed the hydros off, but he was only pretending.

"Fooled you," he said, grinning. I glared at him, started the reel again, and stood fuming as the net came in, my hand clenched on the controls. A fish came over the rail. Damon grabbed it. Too slow this time, I did not stop the reel.

"HEY-HEY!" he yelled. "You be careful, now. I don't want to get my hands torn off."

"Sorry," I said. I started it again. A clatter of fish came over the rail. We each took one.

Travis looked at me, annoyed, and pushed me back, dropping his fish in order to take mine. "You run the hydros. We pick the fish."

I stepped away, unsure if he was right, still hoping to please.

"Hey, Rose," Nate called down. "Don't just stand there. Pick fish while you're waiting to reel in."

I took another fish. Travis glared at me and swore. He shook the net until it tore and his fish flew across the deck.

"Okay. I got it." He jerked mine from my hands. I threw up a fist as though to snatch it back, then stopped and stepped away, trying to choke down my rage.

This is stupid, I thought. I braced myself and clenched my hands around the hydraulics as wordless anger built in a slow wave in my chest. But it wasn't just one thing; it had been many things. Dismissals, jokes I wasn't supposed to get, and, at times, even Nate joined in. The men had decided they did not want me here without ever giving me a chance. It hurt the more because the men did not like me. Now I felt conflicted deep inside, not sure what I believed in, not knowing how to defend myself. It was still very hard for me to fight.

Travis shook the fish loose and gestured at me to start the reel again. The last of the net came over the stern. Up on the bridge, Nate started the boat.

"It'll be a while," he shouted down. "We're heading for the line."

We pitched the fish into the hold, then stood to wait, backs to the deck.

"There it is," Damon spoke.

I looked up. He jerked his head to point. "The North Line."

Ahead, a crowd of boats ran down the line where fish heading for the river entered the fishing district. Nate had told me about this place. Fish flooded in here sometimes on a good tide, and when they did, the line became a riot scene of men and metal fighting for sea space. But the boundary itself was invisible, a loran line marked on the charts and drawn on water only by the wakes of the boats running along it.

Nate shouted down, "Keep away from the rail."

Ahead, boats churned the water into a man-made storm. Nate forced his way into the pack and ran full speed along the line, looking for space.

"Keep away from the rail!" he shouted again.

We crunched against another boat and the tires crushed flat, then rebounded, driving us back. The skipper shouted, "Go back where you came from, motherfuckers," and Nate howled back, an inarticulate cry of anger and frustration.

Damon looked at me. "Too rough for you?" he said. He leaned against the rail, showing off. Maybe he wanted to awe me, or humiliate me, or both; maybe I was incidental to the moment. It didn't seem to matter why, but he took a worthless risk looking at me. I bit my lip.

A Russian boat slammed against our side. We shuddered, knocked sideways by the blow, and the boat slid past, its anchor all but grazing Damon's head. He stumbled from the rail, his face gone slack.

I stared at him. He sat up abruptly, rubbing his hand over his head as if to make sure it was still intact.

"Everything okay?" Nate shouted from the bridge.

"Fine," Damon called back, almost angrily, as if to erase his momentary fear.

Nate turned his back. We reached the front of the pack again.

"Let 'er rip!" Nate shouted.

Travis hurled the buoy overboard, and the net raced out. It whipped back and forth as it flew over the stern. Rags of web brushed against my face like ghostly fingers. I ducked away as much as I could, afraid it would drag me overboard.

It caught short. A tearing, ripping sound.

"BACKLASH!" Travis slammed on the brake. Nate cut the throttle. Damon tore the net loose where it had tangled, but another boat seized the chance to set their net directly in front of ours.

"Motherfucker!" Nate yelled. He swung our boat under their stern and finished laying gear inside the line. But two more boats set their nets out between us and open water, cutting us off from the fish.

He rammed the *Shameless* back through the pack. "All right, guys, pick it up fast. We're going to try this again."

We made another set. The net backlashed once more, and we lost our chance.

"What the FUCK!" Nate said. "What's wrong with us?"

He killed the boat and came across the bridge.

Damon ripped the web loose. "Okay," he said.

"Am I clear?" Nate asked, looking at the net. The tide ran hard, carrying us back, and the net had drifted close against our stern.

"Yeah!" Travis said, glancing over the side. Nate threw the boat into gear.

The net sucked in the prop. The engine died.

"Goddamn!" Nate killed the throttle, looked back, and vaulted to the deck. "Goddamn, goddamn it all." His face was tight. "Next time I ask you if I'm clear you make sure I'm fucking CLEAR, okay?"

Travis looked down. Nate kicked open the hatch over the lazaret. Facedown on deck, he knocked out the bolt that opened the inspection plate and reached shoulder deep into the sea to feel the propeller.

"Oh, god," he said. "It's fucking mummified. I hope to Christ I didn't bend something."

He fumbled for his knife and hacked blindly underwater at the mass of web. Another vessel passed; its crew grinned down at us, but we were drifting quickly out to sea, back from the pack. We watched in silence.

In a moment, Nate rolled on his back, rubbing his shoulder.

"Somebody else take a turn, okay?" he said. "I can't feel my hand."

I took the knife from him, lay down and thrust my arm through the inspection plate. The icy water took my breath away. I stretched to the limit of my reach and sawed hard at the wad of net, my face pressed to the soaking deck.

Damon cracked a joke, and the men laughed. I heard them dully, as if from far away.

"Your turn, Travis," Nate said, when mine had passed.

Damon took over after Travis, then Nate again. I stared out to sea. Water and sky met at the edge of sight. No sign of any shore, but, in the distance, a crowd of boats still steamed forward and back along the Line. There were more now than there had been before.

As the sun dipped low, Fish and Game came on the air and announced another opener. I looked at the radio.

"Don't they have any mercy?" I said.

The guys stared at me.

"*Never* hope that they won't give us an opener," Nate said.

"You want me to blow in your ear and give you a fucking refill?" Damon asked. "Bristol Bay is an endurance fishery. This here, this is nothing."

"Yeah," Nate said. "No bitching, okay?"

I didn't answer. I was suddenly afraid that I would cry. I felt so lonely, foolish, and tired. I wish Damon and Travis had never come, I thought. The work had been easier when I was the only deckhand because I'd been happier then and there'd been no one to bully me. Even Nate had changed. He now seemed always on the verge of rage.

Once we got the last of the line out of the prop, we ran out to fish again. The rhythm of setting out, towing, running, and picking up the net blurred in my mind until I was conscious only of weariness. At midnight, when the district closed for fishing, we picked up for the last time and delivered our catch. We had less than a thousand pounds. It was two in the morning by the time we reached the river.

We'd missed the last announcements for the day. Nate called Fish and Game on his cell, and held the phone up so we could hear as the message played in the empty office.

"Wonder what the average was," Damon said.

"That's what I'm wondering."

The canned voice of the Egegik announcer came over the air. ". . . and in Egegik, a seven thousand pound average catch was recorded today . . ."

"What the fuck? Seven thousand pounds?" Travis said.

"Must've been killing 'em on the North Line in the afternoon," Nate said. "Goddamnit. I kind of thought so when I saw those boats." I looked at him. He stared into space, biting his lip. The other men looked at each other and grinned sourly. Damon went out to piss, came back in, and crawled into his bunk. Travis followed. But Nate continued to sit bolt upright in the captain's chair, his fingers beating an anxious rhythm against the wheel. He made no move to go to bed.

I finished putting the dishes away, set up the coffee pot, and lay down.

"Are you coming?" I asked Nate.

We slept in our clothes and the bunk was cold, but at night I would hold him as we collapsed asleep. It was our only moment of contact in the day, and it was the sweeter for being so brief. Tonight, though, he did not join me, and the look on his face kept me half-awake with concern for him.

"Yeah, okay. Gotta get some rest, I guess," he said at last. He stood up and crawled into the bunk. "I was just wondering if I ought to go upriver tonight or not. Seems like maybe we could do well up there with a first set. Maybe not. God, I'm so mad we missed those fish today. But it's early yet. The season's long. We can make it up . . ."

"Uh-huh." I had begun to drop off.

"I gotta do better than this. Mark is counting on me. You're counting on me. Hell, I'm counting on me. We've just got to find fish."

"Tomorrow," I slurred. "It'll be okay."

"All right, I'll stop talking. You can sleep." Nate wrapped his arm around me. "You all right?" he said.

I tried again, but was too tired to answer. The world slipped away from me. I felt like I was falling, and then I did not even feel.

EIGHTEEN

⁓

THE NEXT MORNING, fog piled heavily on the horizon over swells of glaucous, almost greasy-looking water. Nate steered for the West Line, the farthest from the shore. Soon the land disappeared behind us. Then there was nothing but that gray water and the fog moving ever closer.

Just inside the boundary we found fish and followed them, waiting for the opener. Other boats gathered, crowding us until we lost our position. When the clock struck, we had no room to lay our net. Boats on all sides of us set out, lacing the water with gear. Nate drove in and out between them, moving fast, looking for space. Moments slid by, unrecoverable.

"Look at that guy's net," Damon said. It lit up with spray as the fish struck it. Another boat set out in front of the first, cutting him off. "Uh-oh, corked him. That's what shotguns are for . . ."

"Let 'er rip," Nate shouted down, too late.

Damon flung the buoy, and our net poured over the stern. Nate towed a moment, then had us buoy it. He ran its length, killed the throttle, and came on deck.

"'Bout time we got our net in the water," Damon said.

Nate didn't hear him. "I was listening to the VHF, to the guys who went upriver last night," he said. "Sounds like it was pretty hot up there. If we'd've gone I bet we'd've gotten ten thousand pounds." He shrugged. "It's too late now. Anyhow, there's not much left around here." He turned back to the radio.

The fog came down as we brought in that first set. I had my back to the sea, stooping to pitch fish into the hold. I felt the chill breath preceding it and the darkness falling as it cut us off from the sun. I straightened to find the boat wrapped in gray mist. Color and sound drained from the world.

"I can't see a goddamn thing," Nate cursed softly from the bridge. He scrambled down the ladder onto the deck to watch the radar as he steered. In a moment he stuck his head out again and told us to wait. We were headed into the river mouth to make a set for fish ebbing with the tide. But after a moment of steering blind, he said we wouldn't lay out again until he could see where we were.

The three of us crowded into the cabin, the steam from our wet rain gear thickening the air. We drifted, moving just fast enough to maintain steerage. The water grew crowded, boats appearing and disappearing in the mist. In the river mouth, we passed through the tender anchorage and saw the *Rogue* with three nets shrouded about her. Web and fish hung from her anchor chain.

"I guess a couple people hung their nets up on one of the tenders," someone said over the radio.

"Yeah. I heard some crazy fucker saying he's going to sue the company. Fucking, don't fish in the tender anchorage," came an answer.

"It's thick out here. Can't set out when you don't know where you are."

"Yep. True enough."

Their voices were replaced by others. Two boats had collided on the North Line in the fog. One of them was taking on water. The crew was trying to save it with a pump. The other boat stood by, trying to help, but the water got ahead of them too fast. Finally, the men abandoned ship. It sank with a rush, leaving the mast still sticking out of the shallow water.

"Fuck, that'll be a hang-up," someone said.

Nate nodded. The men had fallen asleep where they sat. Still, we idled blindly through the fog, drinking stale coffee to stay awake.

Midmorning, the fog lifted as quickly as it had come, shredding in a sudden gleam of light. Nate followed the low curve of the beach north, watching for fish. He laid the net out close against the shore. We had a few good clatters as we set out and drifted slowly out to sea, picking the net a shackle at a time so the bulk of it was always in water.

We were carried toward the North Line by the tide. Soon, I saw the mast of the boat that had gone down. It loomed forlornly out of the gray-brown water. Other fishermen had set their nets around it. I watched numbly as they worked their gear.

I had slipped into that stage of exhaustion where logic runs backward, looking-glass fashion, and emotions eddy in strange currents. My body seemed to move erratically, disconnected from volition. I saw it as if from far away, smaller and weaker than the others, but a body only, like all the rest.

"Try one here," Nate yelled.

We set our net, but no fish hit and it came back empty. Farther down, we tried again, but there was nothing.

"Fucking water hauls," Damon said. He crouched on deck and began to dismember a fish lying at his feet that had been left on deck from earlier in the day. He tore its head off and slid his hand inside. "Hello. I'm a dead motherfucker," he said, working its mouth.

Travis laughed. "Let me see that," he said. He pushed its eyeballs out so that his thumbs came through the sockets and stretched his fingers through its jaw, moving it so that it looked alive. The smell of blood and flesh hung over the deck.

"Hello, I'm dead," Damon said again, stretching the joke. "Last year," he began, and told about a slow day on the Flats, getting too many flounder in the net. He'd shoved seal bombs into their mouths and thrown them overboard to wait for the splash. "Like torpedoes," he said, and his tale sent him and Travis into cramping gusts of laughter.

"Ugh," I said. "Ugh." Sunlight hung over us, its clarity burning the dirty boat, the bright water, and the dark mast in the distance. They ignored me.

"Hey, which is the fucker that wouldn't come out of the net?" Travis asked. He scrabbled through the fish until he found one marked by web. Grabbing its jaw, he flogged it against the rail until it came apart, then dropped its head and hunted for another. The deck grew slick with blood.

Nate stood watching silently from the bridge. "Hey, cut that out," he called at last. "You're acting like fucking perverts."

Travis let go of the fish he held, then lit up in anger, seeing our faces. "If we were catching fish I wouldn't be doing this," he yelled back at Nate, a challenge in his voice that I did not understand.

"Nate's showing off for you," Damon said to me. "Acting all softhearted." He flounced across the deck. "Lalala, I'm a bunny humper," he sang. But Nate had turned back to the wheel.

I hunched down on deck to get out of the wind and closed my eyes. My mind wandered. I jerked it back. It wandered again, and I could not capture it. Meaningless images swirled in my head. I heard voices that said nothing, but muttered endlessly, *tired tired tired tired tired tired tired tired tired*.

Lying there, I felt something strike my face and roll to the ground. I didn't react at first. I felt another soft blow, then another. Slowly, I opened my eyes and met the returning stare of an eyeball lying in my lap. A sea-green eye without a body. It lay with shreds of bloody flesh still attached, unseeing yet somehow seeming to witness this. Dishonored. Gone. Two more lay on the deck beside me. I grabbed them and flung them overboard, rubbing my hands to forget the memory of their touch.

Travis laughed. He sat across from me beside a pile of fish, another eye in his hand, his face expressionless. Beside him, Damon grinned.

I closed my eyes again, not caring now. Wanting only to sleep.

NINETEEN

⌐̴

THAT NIGHT I woke to see Nate standing in the cabin, tapping the barometer as if to make it rise.

"It's going to be fucking shitty tonight," he said when I got up. "There's a front moving in from out west."

That morning, most of the boats anchored up inside the river mouth, but Nate kept fishing, anxious to make up for lost time. We stayed near the coast throughout the day, but that night when Fish and Game extended the opener, Nate headed west, farther out to sea.

"Sometimes you'll get 'em when it blows like this," he said. His eyes were glazed with fatigue. I wondered if he was thinking any longer or if he had just surrendered to the moment.

The rain flogged us as we waited on deck. We bucked west toward open water, into the teeth of the rising gale. Damon stumbled across the deck, pale faced, sweating. I vomited openly, too sick for fear. Nate set the net out on the West Line, but when he tried to run its length, the boat washed over it, skidding down cresting waves. It didn't seem that we were catching much, but in that water it was difficult to tell.

"Fucking hell," I heard him yell, but not to us. He was screaming into the wind.

In half an hour, he decided to pick up. He heard a radio report of fish to the south of us and, on a sudden impulse, determined it would pan out.

Damon and Travis round hauled the net, pulling against the wind and tide. Though they were swiftly exhausted, neither of them would move aside and let me work. It was my job, though, so I stood by until Travis grunted, "If you really want to do something useful, go make me some lemonade."

He was trying to humiliate me. I did as he asked. I thought I had to. But I grew furious as I stumbled through the cabin, struggling to mix the powder and water. The juice box fell to the floor and I scrabbled for it in the pitching, rolling welter of boots and trash on the gallery floor. Tears stung my eyes. I blinked them angrily back. Nausea welled up. I choked it down. Two spoonfuls of juice mix. Fill the bottle with water. A spoon to stir . . . where were all the spoons? . . . if only the boat would stop moving just for a moment . . . skip the bloody spoon, no need to stir. I hurried desperately to get outside.

On deck again, I clutched the rail, quivering for air, then shoved the lemonade in Travis's face. He gulped it down and handed me the jar. At his feet, the net piled up, clotted with dying fish. The others crouched over it in the half dark, tearing out the bodies one by one. I dropped the pitcher and stumbled across the deck, hanging on to the reel. I grasped a salmon, a slim thing mangled by the web. It had passed through layers of net as it died, and the folds of gear thrashed in a tangle around its flesh. With my fingers in its gills I dragged it loose, dropped it, and grabbed another. Alongside me, someone did the same, but in the darkness, glazed with spray, and in the anonymous, orange protective rain gear, I could no longer tell who it was. It could have been Nate or anyone.

As the boat tossed, the fish moved like water, sloshing back and forth. Knee-deep in them, we couldn't keep our footing. Nausea swept over me. I fell and stood, and fell again, still picking fish. Motion for motion, the man beside me mirrored me. When the last fathom of net was cleared and on the reel, I lay down flat on deck. My body rolled with the motion of the sea. Water streamed across the deck, washing over me, but I didn't care.

Nate called my name from the top of the house. Just for a moment, I thought about ignoring him, but I couldn't do that. I got to my knees and crawled up the ladder, clinging to it. I thought that he must have a job for me, but when I reached him he told me to stand beside him with the wind in my face. It would make me feel better, he said.

Maybe it would have if I could have stood, but since there was no work I had to do, I let the strength slip out of me again. I slumped to the floor, leaning against the smokestack. It was almost warm. We were running from the western boundary in search of fish. The night was dark, and we did not pass any boats as we went.

"Must've all quit early, anchored up," Nate said. He brushed the rainwater from his face with his wet sleeve. "Should I check your pulse, Rose? You look mostly dead."

"I'm all right," I said. Remembering what Everett had said on the *Arctic Storm*, I added after a moment, "I'm a deckhand. I don't need no doctor." I was trying to joke, to wipe the look of overstrain off his face, but instead it came out sounding foolish.

"You don't seem all right. It was round hauling that did us all in. I never should've done it in this shit. Shouldn't even've been out here. But Christ, you never know until you try."

"Un-huh."

"Listen, what about we call it a night, go and deliver?" he asked, looking down at me. I didn't answer. Dimly, at that moment, I believed he would do whatever I needed of him.

"I shouldn't be doing this," Nate said half under his breath. He swung the boat toward the river mouth. "I'm letting Mark down . . . fuck . . . if he was here he wouldn't be quitting. But you'll feel better soon. I promise."

As he changed course to ride with the waves, the motion of the boat grew easier. My sickness subsided. In a little while, I crawled to my knees again, then stood beside him. The wind stung our faces, hard, heavy with water and salt. It tasted almost like blood.

"Thanks," I said, quietly. He didn't seem to hear.

In the darkness ahead, I could see the yellowish glare of the sodium lights, men running across the tender, and the flash of spray crashing high against its hull. As we drew closer, the swell slammed between our boats, breaking into confused seas. Damon clung to the bow, waiting to catch the line as the crewmen flung it. It fell between the boats. They hauled it back and tried twice more before he lunged forward, grabbed it, and made it fast.

"Let's make this quick, guys," Nate said. "Get the fuck away from here." He waited by the rail for his chance and swung across onto the tender, our fishing license clenched between his teeth. The tendermen lowered the scale. Travis caught it and struggled to attach the hook to a brailer of fish, but the boat, pitching, jerked it from his grasp. The steel scale swung past his head. I grabbed it and clutched it to my chest, but its motion was too violent to control.

Travis looked up at me. "Can't you even hold the fucking scale still? I'm about to get my fucking head bashed in here," he shouted.

The boat rose to another swell. The hook slipped in and the crane lifted the brailer from our hold.

Nate came to the rail. "Get . . . Fuel . . ." he shouted. I ran into the cabin and grabbed the fuel key, but as I turned the lines snapped tight. The boat lurched. I fell against the reel. The key fell from my hand and slid across the deck.

I tried to grab it.

"Hurry!" Nate shouted. Travis swore and flung me out of the way, groveling for the key himself. I stood back up, clutching it, and shoved him. Suddenly, I was blind with rage at him, the boat, fishing, and the night itself.

"Look, cocksucker, I already know you don't think I can do anything," I snarled. "You don't need to act like this." I had more to say, days' worth of frustration and humiliation to curse out at him, all the times he'd pushed me out of the way to answer back to, but I was stopped midstride by the look on his face. He looked shocked, childishly hurt.

"I never said I thought you couldn't do anything. I . . . I . . . I never . . ." he stuttered in a small voice. Then he stopped speaking, bent, and pulled off the fuel cap. I stared as if I'd never seen him before. The guys on the tender were passing me a fuel hose. Green nozzle for diesel, I checked automatically as I handed it to Travis.

"I'm sorry," I said at last. And it was true. The anger I had cherished was gone, leaving me empty in the moment of speaking it. I no longer hated Travis. Instead, I felt as if I'd been screaming at someone I didn't know.

"Let's forget it," he said. "We all just need sleep." He turned his back on me, squatting over the filler hole. I watched him in silence. It took a long time to fill the tank. When he finished, he moved across the deck to the other tank. It occurred to me for the first time that the fault might not have been all on his side, but I pushed that thought away, unable to cope with it yet. For now, we had a job to do.

Travis finished pumping fuel, and I handed the hose back to the tender. The last of my energy had slipped away with my anger. I was conscious only of weariness. I waited until Nate jumped on board the *Shameless* again and turned upriver into calmer water. Then, at last, I went inside and hovered over the oil stove, trying to warm my hands.

The guys had stayed on deck to smoke. Nate and I were alone.

"Come and stand here by me," he said. I leaned against him as he steered. He wrapped his arm around me.

"I thought you and Travis were going to get in a fistfight back there at the tender," he said. "Was that about what I thought it was about?"

"Probably."

"Don't think I haven't noticed the guys picking on you," he said. "There've been times I've wanted to jump down off the bridge and hit Travis in the face so hard he'd be out for a week. But I can't bitch the crew out for you. I can't do a fucking thing. It'd just make it worse in the long run. And you know . . . guys like Travis . . . they just don't like having a girl on the boat." His voice asked me to understand.

I waited for a moment all the same, hoping for something more from him, some acknowledgment, maybe, that they were wrong, or that he at least did not believe that a woman's work was worth less than a man's. But it wasn't forthcoming. I tried not to let it matter to me.

"It's okay," I said. I tried to believe he was right. There was nothing he could do. I leaned on his shoulder anyway. "The guys aren't so bad. If I keep on, sooner or later they'll get used to me. If I keep on . . . I guess I'm not so sure I can anymore."

"You know what, Rose? Damon gives me shit every time I make a decision. But there's a reason I'm skipper and Damon isn't. I gotta let it go. You gotta let it go. They're assholes. Whatever. We have a job to do."

"Yeah?"

"Yeah. There's something else I want you to remember . . ." he went on. "Travis . . . Mark gave him a job to get him out of shit back home. I'd guess he had a tough place to grow up. So . . . bear with him?"

"Jesus Christ." It seemed briefly to be too much to ask.

"Just bear with him. Okay?" He let go of me and slowed the boat, looking for a place to anchor up. Damon stuck his head in the door. Nate sent him out on the bow to drop the hook.

When Travis came in, I looked at him with half-unwilling empathy. In a way it was true, I thought. I didn't know him at all. He'd been my enemy and that was all. When he had stammered out his hurt denial, I'd seen him for the first time as a person. Now he stared at me, his eyes confused. He nodded when our eyes met.

"You all right?" I said, as softly as I could. I wanted badly for things to be at peace between us.

"All right," he answered, and it was almost true.

TWENTY

TWO DAYS LATER, Egegik closed down. The Kvichak River wasn't reaching its escapement, Fish and Game announced. They thought the fish were being intercepted by boats at Egegik.

"How can they tell which river these fish belong in?" I asked Nate.

"Well, the fish we're catching have been fairly small. That's typical of Kvichak reds, so I think it's true that that's what we've been getting. There's a high proportion of two-ocean fish—fish that stay at sea for only two years before returning to the river—in the Kvichak, and they tend to be smaller than fish that spend three or four years out there. I remember one year we fished the Kvichak, and the fish were so small we couldn't catch them. They just kept slipping through the net. But in any case, Fish and Game can't take the chance. They have to make sure fish make it upriver to spawn, so there'll be enough in years to come. I'll show you their numbers . . ." Nate groped for his notebook.

"Hey, you guys want to go into the village and see if we can find a liquor store?" Damon interrupted. "Get some fucking whiskey as long as we're sitting here."

Nate frowned, still looking for his book. "Alcohol and boats don't mix."

"Sure, they mix. Ever meet a fisherman who didn't drink?" Damon said. "We can anchor up and sleep it off."

"Hey, I won't get sick like last year," Travis said. "I've built up my tolerance."

Nate laughed. "Last year we got Travis drunk for the first time. I thought he was gonna die. We tried to stop him, but he just kept going."

"He was sucking it down like mother's milk," Damon agreed. "So, you guys want to get some whiskey? I could sure go for a couple of shotneys."

"Let's do," I said.

"Yeah," Travis nodded. We stared at Nate expectantly.

"Okay. Somebody pull the anchor, we're going to town," he said. "Fuck it, I want a drink, too. I just don't want anything to happen to the boat while I'm running it."

We tied up to a bulkhead inside the river mouth. Nate and I stayed with the boat while Damon and Travis looked for the store. Without them, the boat grew wide, airy, and peaceful. It shifted slowly, rocking at its moorings. The tide was near low and the pilings of the bulkhead towered over us, thick with barnacles and slime. We lay in shadow, but sunlight flashed on the muddy river.

Nate stared at the water. "You know, I hope it takes a long, long time to find that whiskey," he said at last.

He reached out to me, lifted a handful of my hair, and kissed my neck.

"All right?" he said. He wrapped his arms around me, undoing my clothes. The sight of my own body was strange to me. It was paler and more muscular than it had been, but it was the body of a woman still. In that place, it looked soft and even pretty, as translucent and complicated as a shell.

I leaned back into his arms. But the boat jarred with the impact of the men coming back aboard. Hastily, I stepped away again, pulling on my shirt.

They'd brought five plastic liter bottles of a nameless whiskey with them, and a long, loud story about how they managed to find it.

Nate started the engine and headed out into the river to anchor up. Dozens of boats surrounded us. It looked like a carnival under the bright-blue sky, with orange buoys and rain gear for color, and our whiskey the entertainment.

Damon poured us each a shot. "Here's to it and to it again, if you ever get to it and don't do it you may never get to it and do it again."

Nate tossed his shot down, snorted, and wiped his eyes. "That's some bad whiskey."

"Cheap, though. Drink enough and you'll stop tasting it."

"We've sure got plenty."

We started a game of Hearts and played as we drank. The men were drinking hard, but somehow I did not want to join them, though I sat with a glass of whiskey for company's sake. The quiet of the afternoon had stayed with me. Late in the evening, I slipped out on deck to watch the last light leave the sky. Scraps of talk floated out to me:

"The Rices are all big. You should see Travis's uncles. Those motherfuckers are so fucking big. Shoulders like fucking linebackers. And mean."

"We're a fighting family," Travis said.

"I will fly to Washington to help you kick that motherfucker's ass." That was Damon again.

"I'm going to kick his ass. I would've done it before I left, but I didn't want to get fucked up right before fishing. I told him I was gonna kick his ass when I got back." Travis.

The cabin door clicked open. Nate came out on the deck. "I knew I'd rather be with you than in there, drunk," he said. He sat down beside me. But he shifted restlessly, and in a moment he turned to go again. "I'll be back," he said. I knew he wouldn't.

A cold breeze made me shiver. I felt lonely and very far from home.

When I went back inside the men were arm wrestling. Nate grabbed my elbow. "You going to try?" His face shone damp with sweat.

"No."

"I'll show you how." He dragged me onto the bench by the table. He and Damon clasped hands over the table, wrestled briefly. Damon won.

"Here, I'll show you," Damon said. He grasped my hand. "Get your back into it. Don't just try with your wrist."

"No, no that's wrong." Nate pulled my hand out of Damon's. "Like this. Use your shoulder."

Damon glared at him and grabbed his arm. Again they wrestled, and Damon won.

"Damn it, Damon. You're too fucking strong."

Damon grinned. He moved aside to let Travis wrestle Nate. Travis grappled with him, breathing hard. Slowly, Nate forced his arm down.

"Try again," Travis demanded. They locked hands again. Their wrists moved as one above the surface. With a shout, Travis brought Nate's arm down.

Nate stared at him. He slipped his knife out of his pocket. "I could stab you, though."

"Hey, that's a helluva knife." Travis grasped for it. Nate clicked it shut and tucked it out of sight.

"Try again?" he said. Damon moved to let him. I slipped past, got in my bunk, and pulled the blanket over my head. The thud of bodies shook the boat. Nate called for me, but I didn't answer. I lay there trying not to move, almost afraid to be the only woman on the boat.

Late that night, I woke to find him lying beside me, his head buried against my shoulder. When I stirred, he rolled over and lay still.

"Stay with me," he said. "Don't go."

"Where are the guys?" I asked. I could hear shouting, but they sounded far away.

"On deck," he said. "Fuck 'em."

"Are they all right?"

"I don't know," he said. He groped at me again, and again his hand fell back to his side. There was a limpness to his flesh that sickened me, but I tried not to turn away from him.

When I woke again it was morning. He was asleep, snoring heavily. I climbed over him, but he didn't stir. Outside the stuffy fo'c'sle, sunlight poured through dirty windows into a wrecked cabin. The freezer door had fallen open, and food lay melting on the floor. One of Damon's snoose cans had spilled. Tobacco and spit pooled with darkening blood from defrosted hamburger in the low spot on the floor.

"What the hell," I said aloud. I cleaned it up and started coffee. I was thinking of Nate. I'd seen plenty of drunken fishermen, but I'd never seen him the way he'd been the night before. It was as if he'd become a different person, his thoughts running in ways I couldn't understand, and it made me afraid.

Overhead, a helicopter passed by. I heard it go, and craned my head to see it but could not.

After a while Nate got up, stumbled out to vomit, then slumped down at the table, his head in his hands. His hair was matted and greasy. He was sweating out the alcohol. Still, he was the man I knew again and no drunken stranger.

"Oh, god," he said. "What happened last night?"

"I don't know," I said. "I went to bed."

"I didn't get in a fight, did I?"

"Not that I know of." I filled a glass with water and brought it to him. He looked so sick I put aside thoughts of the night before.

"Great. Then this is just a hangover," he said. "I was afraid I'd tried to kill Travis or something."

I shook my head. The helicopter was passing over again.

He gulped down the water and held out his glass for more.

"Please?" he said. I refilled it. He flicked on the radio so that we could listen to the Fish and Game announcements. They were still doing the local news. The announcer was talking about a man who'd drowned in the Nushagak River the night before. The skipper of a fishing boat, he fell overboard and wasn't missed until too late.

"I bet they were drinking," Nate said, listening.

"Alcohol is believed to have been a factor," the radio announcer continued.

"Poor bastard probably went out to take a piss, never made it back inside again," Nate said. He looked at me, then out the window.

"Jesus Christ," he said. He shook his head. "Remind me about this next time I drink when I'm in charge."

I looked out again. Chatter continued on the VHF, voices breaking up in the distance.

Nate turned his attention back to his notebook. On the radio, the local news ended. Fish and Game came on. No opener for Egegik. Instead, the biologist warned that Egegik fishermen might be pulled in river to protect Kvichak fish.

"Jesus," Nate said again. "What a zoo that's going to be."

I nodded. The Egegik office went off the air, and the announcement for Ugashik came on. Eight-thousand-pound average the day before.

"Eight thousand?" I said, startled.

"Must not be many boats down there," Nate said. He scribbled down numbers as he talked, then looked up, chewing on his pen.

"Sounds like that might be the place to be," he said. "Get the fuck out of Egegik, change our luck. Ugashik usually gets a big push of fish all at once. If you can catch it right, be the first boat there, you are golden. You are the king. Of course, there's no knowing when that will be, or if the fish will come . . . but we could use a boost." He kept talking, half to himself.

I looked away, out the window at the coming day. After a while, I found a pencil and figured my crew share. Five percent of net catch, minus food and fuel. I realized I hadn't yet made enough to cover my ticket to King Salmon.

Nate saw me looking at the sheet of paper.

"You all right?" he asked.

"Look at this," I said.

He pulled my figures across the table, glanced at them, and shrugged his shoulders.

"Looks right," he said. "But look at it this way. All we have to do is catch a few more thousand pounds, and after that you're in the black. Try working out what Mark has made this year. He pays out 50 percent in wages to the four of us. His payments on the boat and permit, plus expenses like insurance, repairs, and storage, are close to forty grand a year all told. So far, he's lost thousands on this trip."

"I thought we were doing good. You said so yesterday."

"We're doing okay. Nobody's gotten hurt, the boat still floats, and we've caught some fish. But we're not catching enough to break even. A thousand pounds this day, two thousand the next—it seems like a lot but it isn't, not for the Bay.

"I guess you've never seen Bristol Bay on a good year, so you can't know what's missing. I saw a good season here once. You couldn't quite believe how many fish there were then. You felt like maybe you could walk on water if you stepped over the side. We were being paid more that season, too. Used to be, you'd expect to get more than a dollar a pound. That was what it was like when Mark got into this fishery, and now he can't get out."

"Why not?"

"Who would buy? Besides, if he sold this boat, he wouldn't get enough for it to cover his payments, and he wouldn't have anything at all coming in from the Bay next year. Because if it ever does come back, it could be golden."

"Hmmm." I bit my pencil, understanding something I hadn't wanted to, why Nate was so desperate to find fish. He hated to fail or to let people down, and he loved Mark.

"However," he said, "if we can hit Ugashik just right, intercept the peak of the run there, we may really start catching fish. It's still early in the season, and you don't necessarily expect them to be pouring into the Bay yet. It could still be a good year . . . maybe . . . if I play the cards right . . ." He was dreaming now. "I'm not crazy, Rose. It could happen again."

Damon rolled from his bunk at the sound of our voices. He spat into the sink and gulped some water. "Got any coffee?" he asked. He lifted the empty pot to see, filled it with water and grounds, and put it on the stove, then stood scratching his crotch as he waited for the pot to boil.

"Shit sucks," Damon said at last. There was no answer.

TWENTY-ONE

~

ALL DAY THE Coast Guard helicopter hovered over the river, searching for the body of the man who'd drowned. But all of us knew there was no real hope. The water was too cold and too quick.

The next day they called off the search. Relatives would be notified. That was all. But that afternoon, Mark called the boat. After they talked a while, Nate asked at last, "Say, 'd they ever say who that guy was that drowned? We never heard."

"Some Russian guy, I think," Mark said. "Did you know him?"

"No," Nate said. I heard his voice clearly. We had known the name already, and suddenly I knew that Nate had half hoped we had misheard, as if not knowing it could make it untrue. Not that it mattered, really—he was just a man, like all the others. Someone we hadn't known, now gone for good. I wondered if I'd passed him in the street, stood in line with him in Anchorage. It seemed like there should have been some sign, something to tell us what was about to happen. But there never was.

A silence settled over the boat. Without much discussion, that night we transferred to Ugashik. We arrived there late on the following day, crossing the district boundary near the end of an opener. A handful of boats fished on the line, but as we ran for the tender anchorage, they began to pass us. They were heavy laden, riding low in the water. Nate watched them go.

"Must've been a hell of an opener today," he said at last. "Well, we'll be here in the morning."

We headed into the river mouth to anchor up. The land there was almost as flat as water. It mixed with the water in mudflats and sloughs, so that there did not seem to be any clean break between sea and earth. Far to the south, the horizon was ringed with the mountains of the Alaska Peninsula. They were so distant they had an air of unreality, mountains from another world. Boats crowded around us in the anchorage. They too had transferred into Ugashik over the last few days, waiting for the projected big push of fish.

It was early yet when we anchored, and after eating we sat around the table for a while, not doing anything.

"Look at that guy, he's setting off an emergency flare," Travis broke the silence suddenly. Another boat followed suit. "I wonder what's wrong with those fuckers?"

"It's just the Fourth of July," Nate said. "Don't you remember? They're celebrating."

"I'll be celebrating in a couple weeks, when we've taken on another fifty thousand pounds," Damon said. Nate did not reply. I was silent, thinking of my father. I remembered him holding me up to look at fireworks, years ago in the Wrangell Harbor. Thinking of that, of the reds and yellows of fire over the water, I'd've liked to have heard what he'd thought of fishing.

I pulled out my journal and started a new page, writing to him this time. But after the first paragraph, I closed the notebook. There was too much to say and no time to write it all, even if I'd been able to send a letter. I crawled into my bunk and lay in the stuffy, smelly half dark, wondering why in god's name I'd ever gone fishing and if he'd ever felt the same way.

In the end, he'd quit, after a life spent mostly on the water, and gone up north to work as a laborer in the oil fields. A job he hated, but a job that paid a regular income. My mother needed health care by then, and maybe it was too hard to make it anymore on deck. They did not always get along these days, but they were bound together at the root. He would take care of her, she of him. Though the rest of us might wonder how lives turn out the way they do, how men and women can stray so far afield from their intentions. And after all, they loved each other still.

"Maybe tomorrow things will work out," I thought.

I buried my head deeper in my pillow, as if its pressure could make me stop thinking.

⌐⌐⌐

By six the next morning we were out on deck making sets near the river mouth. The sky had clouded over in the night, and the fishing was poor. By noon it had dried up completely. We picked up and ran north along the coast, looking for fish.

"Guess they must've cleaned 'em up yesterday," Nate said, his mouth tight. "Maybe we'll get 'em next time."

But the following day there was no opener. The biologist explained that he had to get more fish upriver before he could give us fishing time. "We anticipate a return to normally scheduled periods shortly," he said.

On the VHF, men discussed it. "Run must be late," they said. "It happens."

"It is what it is," Nate said. "So, we wait." He took us farther up the river, into the mouth of Dago Creek for shelter. A rotting bulkhead gave us space to tie up, but there was no sign that it was ever used. The land was bare except for a dirt track that headed east along the shore. We wandered down it for a little while, unsure where it led. It seemed abandoned, running out of sight in and out of hollows in the grass. Multitudes of birds swarmed overhead. Their wings flashed in unison as they wheeled, as though they kept time to unheard music. Their cries had a queer loneliness, a sound that made your heart ache without knowing why. I didn't know what birds they were. I didn't even recognize the flowers.

Damon and Travis grew bored quickly and turned back toward the boat.

"Why'd anyone want to live in this godforsaken place?" Damon asked. Travis agreed.

Nate and I kept walking, off the road and down along the beach, glad for a chance to be alone. Here, it was all sky and water, endlessly changing as the sun shifted and the wind combed out water and cloud. Standing on shore, I heard a silence that seemed to stretch forever. Even the occasional human noise from the creek mouth, men shouting and engines starting up, felt lost in the vastness of silence.

When we returned to the boat, we found Damon and Travis deep in a pile of porn magazines.

"Where'd you get those?" Nate asked.

"Traded with a guy off the *Captain Morgan*. We gave him Travis's second-to-last can of snoose." Damon held his up. "What do you think of this gal?" he asked. "Looks like they're trying to make her airtight."

Travis stayed oblivious, hunched over a page, his music blaring.

"I've never seen that color of pink," I said, just for something to say. It was a startling picture, the girl unreal against the backdrop of the dirty cabin.

"Probably Crisco or some shit. To make her look like she's just been fucked." Damon kept his eyes on the picture. "You guys didn't happen to bring me a red head in a leopard-skin thong from the village, did you?"

"Nope," Nate said. Hearing our voices, Travis turned off his music and glanced up. I leaned over Nate's shoulder, reading the caption.

"She likes country songs," I reported. It lessened my discomfort to speak, as if we weren't all in the same boat.

"Jesus, you can't look at that!" Travis cried at me. "It's not right! I mean, Jesus!"

"Hey, Travis?" I said, "Right now I'd read a cereal box for entertainment. So fuck off."

"The copy's sexier anyway," Nate said, his grin lopsided. "All that perky sweetness."

Damon shook his head and turned back to his page.

TWENTY-TWO

⌐∽

THE NEXT MORNING, I was the first to wake. A breeze had sprung up, and the sky had cleared. Light glittered off the shivering water. But there were no fish and we were at a loss.

I turned from the window and sat down. When the men woke, we listened to the announcements. There was no opener. That day passed slowly, then the next and the next. Each morning, Fish and Game announced that they still projected another push of salmon in the river and that once it came we would be allowed to fish. But the days slipped by and nothing happened. The water stayed empty. Without warning, disaster had struck, and in the face of it there was no appeal.

Without fishing, there was nothing for us to do, and nothing new to talk about anymore. The days were featureless, devoid of incident. We sat for hours at the cabin table or lay in our bunks trying to sleep, stunned by the sheer rapidity of the fish's disappearance.

Damon sank quickly into a sour apathy. Standing, sitting, or lying down, Travis shifted constantly, fidgeting, tormented by an explosive energy he had no outlet for. At times he looked up from his magazine and stared around the cabin as though seeking escape, his eyes gone blank with misery, before returning to the page. Both of them were rationing their tobacco, and in their fear of running out they smoked almost desperately. Each time one went on deck, the other did, too. They stood together, hunching their shoulders against the wind, nursing their cigarettes and telling stories.

Once a day, at high water, we tied up to the bulkhead. Nate did it for my sake. But he said little as we walked, only sometimes pointed out something to look at, a flower or a cloud, as if he were trying to entertain a child.

When we returned to the boat, he lay in his bunk staring at the ceiling while I filled page after page of my notebook with scrawled entries and letters that could not be sent. Sometimes, as I sat at the table, I could hear him beat his head against the pillow.

"What's the use?" he said. "You friggin' idiot, Nate."

After the first week, I also believed no good would come of staying. I was waiting only to go home, but I tried not to say so. Nate's responsibility was to fish as long as possible, and I didn't want to make that even harder for him. Besides, I, too, felt a sense of loyalty that made me ashamed of my desperate eagerness to leave. I'd started this. I would finish it.

TWENTY-THREE

⌇

ONE AFTERNOON IN mid-July, we began to talk of transferring back to Egegik. Damon suggested it first. All four of us were playing Hearts around the cabin table, drinking weak, bad coffee because nothing else was left.

"Ugashik's a bust. Guess we'll be heading back to Egegik soon," he said. It was a statement, not a question, but he looked at Nate, anxious lest he be contradicted.

"We can't transfer," Nate said. He grabbed his notebook and showed Damon the numbers he had copied down from the Fish and Game announcements each morning—how many fish had been caught in each district, how many fish were in the rivers, and what was needed to pass upriver to meet escapement in Naknek, the Kvichak, Egegik. He was explaining what Damon already knew but didn't want to believe. We'd waited so long in Ugashik that leaving for another district wouldn't be worth it. The runs had peaked and dwindled elsewhere. At this point, our only hope of redeeming the season was if the projected fish came to Ugashik.

"We still have a chance to break even here—we don't have that chance if we transfer," Nate summed it up. "Believe me, I want to leave as much as you do. I want to convince myself it's the right decision. But I can't."

Nonetheless, later that week he told me he too had begun to think we would have to leave Ugashik. It was a thought born of desperation, made in the belief that there was no way we could salvage the season.

"I don't want the guys to get their hopes up," he said. "But I want to see what's out there. I think tomorrow we'll go out, run through the district and look for fish. If we don't see any, fine. We'll just keep on going. Head north back to Naknek and put the boat away. But if we do see some jumpers, we'll stick around."

"Sounds good," I said, already feeling better. Any action seemed better than none. Back at the boat, Nate announced his plan.

"About time!" Travis said. Damon remarked that it was what he'd suggested days ago. But all the same, all of us were glad.

The next morning we left Dago Creek at high tide, edging over the shallows that were impassable at low water. Damon and Travis returned to their bunks once we were out of the creek. I sat beside Nate as we headed out to sea, watching for fish. It was a cloudy day, the water smooth and flat. Just outside the creek mouth we saw the first jumper, then another. As we ran we saw flash after flash, until we were surrounded. Nate cut the engine, and in the sudden quiet we heard them strike the water all around us. I looked at Nate and felt my heart sink.

"Well, what do you think?" he asked at last.

"I think we'd better stay," I said, reluctantly. "That's a lot of fish."

"Yeah," Nate shook his head. "Fuck, though . . . I just don't know. Fish and Game could wait until all those fish have gone upriver before they give us an opener. But you're right—with that many fish here we shouldn't leave. Not after having waited this long." He sighed, fired up the boat again and turned back toward Dago Creek.

Damon crawled out of his bunk. "What's going on?"

"Heading back to Dago Creek."

"What the? But WHY?" Damon's face went red with anger. He seemed to swell up. For a second I thought he might hit Nate, though Nate was younger and the smaller of the two, nowhere near a fair match.

"Look out the window. See those jumpers? That's why." Nate didn't even look at him.

Damon stared at him, then abruptly sat down at the table, stuck a cigarette in his mouth, and lit it.

"No smoking in the cabin," Nate said.

Damon jerked open the window, flung his lighted, unsmoked cigarette into the water and exploded. "Look, Nate, you know as well as I do that you're wasting time. We're not going to make money sitting here with our thumbs up our asses saying, 'Please, Mr. Fish and Game Biologist, let me catch a fish.' The season's over. Done. Finished. Take the boat back to Naknek, put it away."

"I ain't quitting till the fat lady sings. There are still fish in this district."

"The fat lady's fucking screaming! How loud can she sing? The season's over!"

"I'm not forcing any of you to stay just cause I'm staying. If you want to leave, I'm sure you can find a way to get back to Naknek."

Damon sat silent. He opened his mouth as though to speak. Closed it again. Finally, he pulled out his snoose can. I stared out the window, watching fish splash against the water. Like Travis, I was shifting in my seat, my body longing for something to do. *I could leave*, I thought, *go on to a different life, never see the* Shameless *or her crew again*. It was my own choice to make, or so I told myself.

The phone rang. It was Mark. He shouted into the phone, as he always did, as if that would make it easier for his voice to cover the miles between us.

"How are you doing, Nate? Those fish show up?" His words crackled with static.

"Still waiting," Nate answered.

"Good," he said. "Every time I call I'm scared you'll be back in Naknek, or that you'll tell me it's over, you're going home. Stick it out as long as you can. If you can just get a few more thousand pounds . . ."

He was pleading. I looked at Nate.

"Yeah, we're not ready to quit yet," Nate said slowly. "We'll stick it out, hoping to fish. I've thought some about transferring, but it doesn't seem worthwhile long's there's a chance we'll get a push of fish down here."

"That's what I'm thinking," Mark said. "This can't be the end of the season already. Can't be."

Nate grunted in reply.

"How're the guys? Hanging in there? How's Rose?" Mark asked.

"The guys might be happier if I had a new *Playboy* to give them, or maybe some whiskey," Nate said. "Rose's all right."

"If they get too homesick and start giving you trouble, put 'em on the phone. I'll tell them about my debts," Mark said.

Damon glared at that, stood up, and crawled into his bunk.

"Naw, nobody's ready to mutiny yet," Nate said. "I hope. Anyway, I've been seeing a lot of jumpers out here this afternoon. I figure there's fish coming still."

I thought I could hear relief in Mark's voice as he said good-bye. But when Nate set the phone down, he looked despairing.

"You know, when I heard that ring, I was praying it was Mark, that he would tell us to call it quits. That he needed you guys back on the *Antagonizer*," I said.

"So was I," Nate said.

"Fuck yeah!" Damon growled.

"Fuckin' A! Are we going back to Naknek?" Travis stuck his head, flushed with sleep, out of his bunk.

"Are you fucking kidding? We're going to stay here for the rest of our goddamn lives," Damon said.

"Oh. Fuck. I thought we were in Naknek," Travis said.

Silence.

"Fuck this shit," Damon spoke again.

"Yeah," Travis said.

This time the silence lasted. Nate hunched his shoulders. I thought again of leaving.

The tide was high when we reached Dago Creek. We had run out of propane for the stove, so Nate and I collected what cash we could find and walked down the road to look for a store, carrying the tank between us on a buoy hook. After an hour we reached a handful of cabins, weather-beaten, one-story places clustered on a rise of land. An American flag marked the post office. It looked like a child's drawing—the square-edged buildings all slightly off kilter, perched on the hill of crayon green under a blue and depthless sky. Paths led from house to house. We walked through them until we found the store, a collection of canned goods in a shed outside someone's home. The owner came out of the house to fill our propane tank. We bought a candy bar as well. It was all we could afford.

"I wouldn't mind living in a place like this," Nate said. I nodded. It seemed a place apart from the world, left outside of time.

We left the village and kept on walking along the green bluffs by the sea. Children from the village played on the beach below. They had a four-wheeler, onto which five of them crowded at a time to race up and down the hard-packed beach. A girl of about twelve drove, her long black hair snapping in the wind.

After a time, the track we followed veered inland and headed out across the tundra. We kept walking until we came to a rise where the wind kept the mosquitoes down. There we stopped to share the candy. It was the longest we'd been away from the boat since we'd reached Bristol Bay, and we were weak from inactivity. We'd both grown too thin these last few weeks. Food had been in short supply since we quit fishing.

We sat shoulder to shoulder, glad to be alone. Sometimes the lack of privacy on the boat was hard to bear. Even when Damon and Travis were asleep, the boats anchored alongside the *Shameless* could see into our cabin, and the open country made it impossible to walk out of sight of the fleet. The night before, we had pulled our blanket over our head.

"Stop, stop," I'd whispered. I could hear Damon turning the pages of his magazine, an arm's length away. But Nate would not stop, and at last I stopped trying, thinking it was louder, and more humiliating than the alternative. I did not know what to do. We kept kissing and whispering in the stifling dark. I wished I was elsewhere, and still I cared for the man with me.

"Can I?" His hand slid up my thigh.

"Maybe . . . no . . . no," I said again.

He stopped at last when Damon began to cough loudly, on purpose. I felt the grim weight of his frustration, and even then I knew that it was wrong that I'd felt as if I had no choice.

And all the same, though I couldn't explain it, I'd drawn ever closer to him. His steadfast determination to finish his job had won my respect. But this closeness remained unspoken. We talked of everything except each other. But I knew we both believed we would be parting soon, unable to find a life that we could share. Parting seemed built into the fabric of this life. And in the last few weeks, the bloom had gone off my wilderness, while Nate himself seemed to have turned inward.

Still, I sighed and stretched my legs, the restlessness of the past days draining out of me. The wind was picking up, whirling dust into our eyes. It never slackened pace here but raced on from nowhere into nowhere with a whisper of half-heard words. Now it carried the lonesome cries of birds and the deep sea smell of salt and water. In this place, human fate was as simple and unknowable as the elements. Nate's hand in mine was quick with life, and life was beautiful.

"We'd better get back to the boat," Nate said after a time. "Tide's falling. I don't want to leave Damon in charge for too long . . ."

Reluctantly, I stood and moved on.

As we reached the road again, an old Ford truck pulled up

alongside us, and the driver offered us a ride. Nate wanted to, so we climbed in.

"Fishermen?" the driver asked. "Me, too. I live in the village, Pilot Point."

We told him about our trip out of the creek that morning.

He said, "I saw a hundred boats go dry trying to get out of Dago Creek once. Short-notice opener at low tide. All those boats went aground, one after another, just a few feet from open water. Missed the fish completely." He laughed, blowing a lungful of smoke out the open window. Sunshine and dust filled the cab of the truck.

"Yeah, I think I'm going to anchor outside tonight," Nate said.

The man dropped us off at the bulkhead where the road ended. The tide was low. No boats but ours lay tied up to the pilings.

"Oh, fuck." Nate ran out to look. The *Shameless* lay grounded on a bank of silt filmed with river water. "Why the fuck didn't Damon move off when the boat started to go dry? . . . I don't know how steeply the bank falls away here . . ." He swung down the ladder as he spoke. As he stepped on deck the *Shameless* shifted until she canted away from the pilings, hanging against her tie-up lines.

"Son of a bitch!" he cried.

I started down the ladder.

He shouted, "Wait." Running to the bridge, he grabbed a line, made it fast, and threw it up to me. "Tie that off. It'll back up the other lines."

I did, although it did not seem that it could help. He scrambled for another. When it was fast, I started down the ladder.

"Be careful," he said. "Don't walk heavily." He felt the straining lines. "If she falls, we'll lose her. But all we can do is wait for the tide."

I stood, feeling the boat quake underfoot, strange and unstable.

"I wonder where the guys are? I shouldn't have cursed at Damon like that. It was my fault for staying away so long."

Treading gently, I followed him into the cabin. Inside, the angle seemed more pronounced.

Damon stuck his head out of his bunk.

"Boat gone dry?" he said cheerfully. His bad mood seemed to have passed over.

"Yeah."

"I figured it might before you guys got back." He swung his legs out of bed and landed heavily on the floor. "Fu-uck. Cabin tilted like this, makes me feel like I'm drunk. Wish I was." He shook a cigarette from Travis's pack, stuck it between his lips and went on deck.

Travis poked his head from his bunk, his hair rumpled in sleep. "Boat gone dry?" he asked.

"Yeah," Nate said again.

Travis jumped out of his bunk, his feet thudding onto the cabin floor, and went outside. The boat lurched as he crossed the deck to piss, came inside to grab a cigarette, looked for a lighter, sat down, stood up, and headed out on deck for a smoke.

"Look, could you just hold still?" Nate said at last.

Travis looked shocked. "Well if you don't want me, I'll just go sit up on the bulkhead," he said. Nate was silent.

"I'll go sit on shore," Travis repeated. He stalked out of the cabin. The boat shuddered as he stepped onto the bulkhead ladder.

"Thank god," Nate said quietly.

Damon stuck his head into the cabin. "I think Travis's running away from home," he said. "He's sitting up there on the bulkhead."

"Good use for him," Nate said. But in a little while he went out to talk to him. I heard their voices, then strained laughter as they searched for common ground.

I stood apart at the cabin door, afraid to sit down. The restlessness I had left behind had rushed in on me again with the sour smell of the boat and men. Again I stared at the water, as though it had something to tell me. Ripples chased over the surface, driven by the wind. I tried to find a pattern in their movement but could not.

TWENTY-FOUR

⟞

OVER THE NEXT few days our hopes that had revived died away again. It was long past the time when the fish should have come if they were coming at all, and there were no more reports of sockeye in the bay, waiting to commit to the river. The fish we'd seen seemed to have simply vanished. Dago Creek had emptied out, too. Only a handful of boats remained. Those who left Ugashik were giving up and going home.

Nate and I kept walking down the shore every day. Though in our hearts we both believed the fish were gone, we talked as if they still might come. Nate blamed himself for the decision that had brought us to Ugashik, and once he offered to give me his crew share if I needed money. When I refused, he said he'd offer it to Mark. Each day he talked through the situation as if it were new, but each time he reached the same conclusion. There was nothing we could do but wait until waiting became absurd.

One afternoon in late July, Mark called to say he needed to fly one of the men back to Cordova to work on the *Antagonizer*.

"Which one?" Nate said. They both looked up, staring at him in hope.

"Damon," Mark said.

Travis dropped his eyes. He seemed to shrink inside himself.

"Think of it like being in jail," Damon said, grinning, when Nate hung up. "One of these days you'll get out, too. God, I can't fucking wait. I'm going FISHING! Going to leave this motherfucking mud circus and make money." He jumped up to cram his gear into his duffel, sweeping his bunk empty.

"Easy, killer," Nate said. "You ain't leaving 'til the morning."

"I don't care. Fucking sit on my bag all night if I have to." He grinned at Travis again for a reaction. "Suckers."

Travis didn't answer. It was as if finding out that Damon was preferred had knocked the last of his bravado out of him.

"Let's mutiny," I said to Travis, only half in jest. "We can tie Nate up and go back to Naknek right now." He shrugged morosely.

"We're mutinying," I told Nate. "I don't know why I never thought of it before."

"I wish you luck," he said. "Untie me in Naknek and I'll buy you a beer."

The next morning, we took Damon to the bulkhead. Travis lay half-awake in his bunk, waiting for him to go. But before he left, Damon leaned down into the bunk and shouted in his ear.

"Just wanted to make sure you realized I was leaving this dump," he said. Travis grunted, rolled over, and buried his head.

"Asshole," he muttered. Damon grinned. He climbed onto the bulkhead and sat on his duffel, waiting for the pilot.

"Fuck him," I said.

"Yeah," Travis spoke from his bunk. It was the first time he'd ever agreed with me.

TWENTY-FIVE

TWO DAYS AFTER Damon left, Nate gave up. He said we'd leave on the next tide.

Not an hour later, Fish and Game announced that the fishery would open in the morning. The fish had moved upriver at last. All along Dago Creek, deckhands shouted and let off flares in celebration. But there was no joy on the *Shameless*. The opener had come too late. All we wanted to do was leave. We suspected, too, that the fish in the river were the last of the season, and that we would find nothing left to catch. Sure enough, the following morning we got up three hours before the opener and drove through the whole district without seeing a single fish. I felt like crying, seeing that.

At last, we found a small school and hung with them until the opener. When we laid out our net we got a few hits, but the fish were so sluggish we couldn't chase more in. When we pulled the net we found that they were already changing to their spawning colors, half-dead and rotten before we even caught them. We would have headed home after that first set, but we'd missed our tide. So we kept fishing, without catching.

By midafternoon Nate didn't have the heart to keep trying. It was so clear that the run was over, and we had failed even to meet Mark's expenses.

"Pick it up," he said. "We're calling it a season." At that moment he looked as Jay had looked, defeated and old beyond his years.

The wind began to rise as we brought the net in. By the time we reached the tender, the sea had grown too rough to tie up easily. After we delivered, we anchored outside of Dago Creek. We meant to leave on the next low water and ride the flood tide north to Naknek. But by nightfall the boat was pitching so hard that Nate moved us inside the creek. I knew that meant we couldn't leave before another change of the tides, if then.

The next day dawned wet and gray. The men lay in their bunks without sleeping. I looked out the window at the line of breakers on the bar.

"Wanna play cribbage?" Nate said at last. We played cheerlessly.

"I sure wish I knew what the average was this season," Nate said, interrupting me without realizing it. After one game he crawled into his bunk again and lay staring at the ceiling.

In the early evening the wind began to die, though the sea stayed rough with a residual swell. I sat watching out the window, willing the wind to keep on falling. It was getting dark already, under a sky heavy with clouds. I knew that soon we wouldn't have enough water to get out of the creek.

Nate spoke to me from his bunk. Looking down, I realized he was watching me.

"What was that?" I asked.

"You want to leave, huh?"

"Kind of. It looks like the weather might be blowing itself out," I said.

Nate got up and looked outside. He looked at me again and bit his lip in painful indecision. "I wish I could see what the water looks like outside the creek," he said.

"You could try standing on top of the house."

"Naw, fuck it. Pull the goddamn anchor. We're leaving," Nate said, suddenly angry. "Hurry up! There's barely enough water as it is. We'll be lucky if we so much as get out of this fucking creek."

It was bitter cold outside and raining hard. I threw the switch on the anchor winch and started bringing in the chain. It came up rattling, heavy with foul mud. Nate banged on the window to tell me to slow down, but he was too late. I had overestimated how much line we had out, and the anchor came running up full speed. It slammed against the bow and swung high on deck, thrown by the force with which it struck the boat. I had been kneeling, and the anchor passed before my face.

I knelt back, shaking. I knew I'd nearly killed myself. I looked in the window at Nate. He was glaring at me. I tied the anchor down and went inside.

"Turn off the hydraulics," he said.

"Oh." I hit the switch by the door, my hand still unsteady. Already, we were drifting quickly down toward the creek mouth, past the few remaining boats. I watched as we passed, through a window half-obscured by rain.

"I can't see a damn thing," Nate cursed quietly to himself. Abruptly, he ran out the door. I heard his feet thud on the roof as he took control from the bridge. The boat touched bottom with a long dragging shudder, but we kept moving. The water grew deeper.

Out of the shallowest part of the creek, Nate came back inside. His anger seemed to have passed over.

"Brrr!" he said. "I thought I'd freeze to death up there. Can you find me something to eat, Rose?"

"Bread and cheese?" I asked. "I could grill it."

"Sounds good," he said.

"That's lucky, cause that's all there is," I said. He pulled me to him and hugged me. Ahead, we could see the line of surf breaking across the river mouth. It looked nasty, even at a distance.

"It'll be calmer once we get outside the bar," Nate said.

Travis crawled from his bunk, scratching his head. "We leaving?" he asked.

"I hope," Nate said. Travis sat down at the table just as we reached the river mouth. The cups and magazines on the table began to slide. He spread his arms to catch them, but it was too late.

"Better sit down," Nate said to me. I threw the food into the cupboard, sat down, and hung on. The boat stood up to meet the breaking waves that seemed to rise up, up over us and smashed against the hull. There seemed no end to them. I wondered why Nate didn't turn back. But we had passed the point of no return.

No one said a word. Travis's grin seemed to have frozen. I tried to imagine I was somewhere else. A strange kind of calm slipped over me. It all seemed to happen so slowly, almost gently, an eternity slid by in that moment.

When the last breaker came, for a long moment we could see nothing but the green muscles of water as it mounted before and above us. It broke as it rose, and I saw, immediately, clearly, how the *Shameless* could roll under its crest, that the weight of the water could smash our windows and surge inside the cabin. We rose to it, and I braced myself. But it passed by, leaving us in deeper water.

"Jesus," said Nate. "I'll never try that again. I wasn't real worried until that last one, but it scared me."

"Uh-huh," I said. I felt as if the swell had taken some part of me with it when it broke.

"You okay?" he said. "You're white as a sheet."

"Yeah, I'm fine," I said. I stood up and put the food back on the counter. That was all.

After the men finished eating I lay down, bracing myself against the roll of the boat. Two hours later, Nate gave the wheel to Travis. I woke for a moment when he got in the bunk.

"How are things?" I asked.

"Pretty good," he mumbled, his face pressed in my hair. "For about a minute this evening I could've killed you though. When that last breaker came, I mean, because I never would've left the river except I didn't want to disappoint you. You looked so hopeful."

"I'm sorry."

"Wasn't your fault," he said. "I should've known better than to leave—I did know better—and you wouldn't've thanked me if I'd drowned you." His voice caught. "Hey, is it okay if I sleep here again tonight?"

"Course," I said.

"Course? I wonder sometimes." He crawled under the blanket. "I wonder sometimes. I wake up in the morning, and I wonder how much longer it'll be before you leave me. You'll go back to the city or to outer-fucking-Ethiopia or somewhere, and I'll never see you again. I should tell Travis to slow down the boat. You can't quit before we reach Naknek."

Abruptly, he rolled away from me and pressed his body to the wall.

"You should try to get some sleep before your wheel watch," he said, his voice muffled by the blanket. "It's not bad steering out here. But if anything happens, if anything changes, wake me up. Hell, I probably won't even be sleeping."

Travis called my name an hour later. I dropped out of the bunk and took the wheel. The swell was coming from behind us now, pitching us forward and burying the bow. I could see nothing but the metallic gray gleam of water in the dark, and the crests of waves pushing past our side. I had no landmarks, nothing but the GPS with its slight delay that left me second-guessing myself, oversteering, understeering, as the boat veered back and forth.

It was the first time I had ever run the boat in complete darkness or in rough seas. I remembered a story from back in Haines about four boys I'd gone to high school with, three brothers and their friend, running a long-liner home at the season's end. A rogue wave knocked them down, and they lost the boat. One of the boys was never found.

Things happen like that. There was nothing anyone could do. But as I thought about it, I grew afraid. It was not a sharp, brief anxiety, easy to forget in the press of work, but a fear that was almost like awe—a cold feeling deep in my chest that grew bigger and did not go away. I was afraid of the ocean and what it could do to me, afraid to be in charge and unable to evade the responsibility. I knew that if I were to disappear into the sea, the sea itself would not change, and I thought again of how Everett had called it God's country.

I kept sitting there, watching the screen of the GPS glow bright green in the dark. The little arrow that meant our boat moved slowly down the faint lines of the coast, shifting as I fiddled with the wheel, trying to compensate for the waves and the current. I watched the GPS, the radar and the compass, each with their night light and their own set of coded information. Slowly, I relaxed, and as I did I learned the trick of feeling the boat, responding to its unseen motions with the wheel so that I used the instruments only as a reference point. I steered a straighter course then, but I was no less afraid.

The sky was brightening over our starboard side before my watch was over, the coastline dividing itself out of the dark. I saw at first the outline of a hill, and then what seemed for a long time to be mist until it hardened into the gray face of a bluff. The curve of the shore and a wisp of cloud stood out. Steadily the light grew clearer, picking out now more clouds and the reach of the shore until there was nothing left unseen in the whole stark landscape. It was as if the world were being created for the first time, with only me for a witness. Water, sky, and land alike were empty of life. Nothing moved but the waves surging past us, their strength subsiding with the dawn.

I woke Nate at four-thirty in the morning. "We've made good time," he said. "We're coming up on Egegik now."

I crawled into my bunk and dozed off. Once, I opened my eyes to see Travis at the wheel again and Nate beside him.

"What's happening?" I asked, trying to drag my thoughts together.

"We're coming into the Naknek River. The season's over. Go back to sleep."

But when we reached Naknek we anchored in the river. The

next tide high enough for us to haul the boat out of the water wasn't until five o' clock the next morning. So began another day of sitting and waiting, this time with the certain knowledge of defeat to wear on us, increasing our restless eagerness to be gone.

At flood tide in the afternoon we tied up to the barge and went ashore for showers. The boatyards along the river were already filling with boats put away for the winter, their windows covered and blank. There was no trace of the cheerful human bustle that had crowded the yards at the beginning of the season. A single man called hello as we passed.

"How'd it go?" he shouted.

"We went to Ugashik," Nate called back.

"You were part of that mess, were you?" he said. "Did you make enough for your tickets home?"

"No," Travis called. The man laughed.

It was a long walk into town. The road was dusty and hot, lined with fireweed already going to seed. I had not seen it bloom, and for a moment I felt cheated. I'd missed summer somehow, without knowing it.

After showering we went to the Red Dog Bar: Crown for Nate and Travis, a beer for me. It was noisy, though few people were there. Lighted signs flickered on the walls. I got out a pen and figured our crew shares on the bar napkin. After all our work, my share was less than my airfare to Naknek had been. I pushed the napkin away.

"Let's not talk about that," Nate said.

Looking over, I saw his face set in a scowl, under the glare of the Miller High Life sign. Travis picked up his glass, reached over, and clicked it against Nate's, half raising it. Nate drank with him. I followed. We sat quietly, shoulder to shoulder. The bartender glanced at us and moved to the far end of the bar. After one drink we got up and left.

Once we reached the boat again, I climbed up on the bridge to think alone. Before the season ended in this way, I'd meant to go back to Cordova, to look for a job that would carry me through until fall. But in a month or two, when fishing was over—where would I go then? I'd thought sometimes of going back to school, on to another place and another life, but in truth that didn't appeal to me as it once might have, even if it was possible for someone as broke as I was. Loneliness seized me, and the old distress at the thought of too many people crowded into airless classrooms and streets.

A school of beluga whales fished in the river, flashing bright-white bodies out of muddy water. In the cabin, Nate and Travis were talking about seining. An hour ago, Nate had been in a black depression. But now Bristol Bay was over. It was time to go seining, and he was almost excited once again. Listening to him, to the current of happiness in his voice, I realized it would break my heart, too, to leave this work behind me. If I quit fishing, I knew that I would leave a part of myself behind on the water. When it stormed at night I would wake to wonder how it was out on the ocean, if Nate was safe. On clear mornings I'd wish that I were out there with him.

The adventure I'd sought had been sadder, dirtier, and harder than I'd dreamed, but all the same, I believed I'd fallen in love with it and with him. I wanted all of it, the sunshine and the water, sea and wind, bad days and good days also. I didn't think I could forget this wild existence to pick up again the threads of an ordinary life. It was real enough for me, and hard enough, and vivid enough. And I felt there was a place for me here.

Looking back, I think now I did not really know what I was choosing when I chose. Only, there were small decisions to be made, and somehow these had added up into the great decisions that shape a life. Somehow, I had become a fisherwoman. I understood the watershed moments on that journey only once they were in the past, and then I did what I could to explain them. As if "I fell in love" could ever be an explanation.

But I was, fatally, a little proud to have succeeded, to still be here—a kind of raw pride at not having quit. It took courage to do this, and maybe that was what I'd sought all along—a clear and physical reason to be brave, real work to do, the strength to do it, and the knowledge at the end of the day that we'd done it together.

And would that suffice? To make a life?

The belugas had moved in nearer to the boat. Watching them, I felt a spurt of envy. Their fates were simple; they did what they were born to do. They made their living in the water, and then they died. Moving quietly so as not to bother them, I went back into the cabin, sick of the company of my thoughts.

The men were drinking beer, dealing out a game of cards. They shuffled and re-dealt so I could join them. We sat until dark, playing as we always did, as if the game were the most important thing in life.

Near midnight, the men crawled into their bunks. We would be hauled out before noon the next day. I went on deck before I followed them. It was nearly dark now, the wind blowing hard. I watched a while before I realized I wasn't alone. Nate slumped on the bridge in the skipper's chair.

He looked up at the sound of my footsteps.

"I couldn't do it," he said. "I couldn't make it pay . . ." He stopped. The tide was turning now. Intermittently, the current rocked the boat. I put my hand on his shoulder and squeezed it. Maybe that was the real watershed moment. He buried his head in my shoulder, and I felt such a wave of tenderness. We were so young still, and cared so much, even the hard times had grace.

"You keep trying, though, because you can't stop . . ." he said.

TWENTY-SIX

AT NOON, RALPH pulled us out with his tractor and put the *Shameless* up on blocks. We spent hours winterizing it again, undoing everything we'd done in June. The men didn't talk much. Nate went in and out of the cabin, slamming the door as if he were closing it on a season's worth of failures.

By late afternoon our work was done. We left Naknek in the truck, hoping to fly standby on the next plane out of King Salmon. At the airport, the line for the check-in counter snaked out of the building into the street. Everyone was trying to get home. We took up our places at the end, squatting on our duffle bags.

After a while Nate went to call Mark. He came back later looking troubled.

"There's an opener day after tomorrow in the Sound. Mark says he wants the *Relentless* and the *Antagonizer* to head over together. He's waiting until I get there, then we'll take off straight away. He told me to be on tonight's flight from Anchorage to Cordova."

"He doesn't have space for me?"

"No."

"So I won't be seeing you once we leave here?"

"It doesn't look like it," Nate said. "Rose, we haven't talked about it, and there won't be much time now. But will you stick around at the end of the season? Go fishing again?"

"I will," I said.

He crushed my hand. "I'll see you then."

The line moved. We settled back in place, sitting so that our shoulders touched.

He said, "I asked Mark if he'd heard of anyone looking for a deckhand, but he hadn't. He's been spending most of his time on the boat."

"Guess I'm back to walking the docks."

"Do you have enough money for a while, if you don't get a job soon?"

"I'll be fine," I said. "One way or another."

That night I stood in the street in Cordova, watching as the *Antagonizer* left the harbor with Nate on board. It grew smaller, until it passed from sight around Salmo Point. I waved until he disappeared, but it was no use. He was gone.

I couldn't have known then that we would marry, how short our happiness would be, or how long and sad and bitter the aftermath. Nor could I have known that in the end it would all have seemed worth it even so, even the mistakes, missed chances, and burnt-out days. That love is worth it, even if it ends.

Instead, at that moment there was only ocean, darkening under the fading summer light. And still, I stood wanting to go to sea, as if to find something unreachable.

After a time, I walked back to the waterfront.

EPILOGUE

LATE NIGHT IN March, I went down to the Cordova harbor to help cut bait on the *Frisian Lady*. The skipper, Gus, was going out long-lining. I helped his brother and their crewmen chop herring in the bait shack on the deck. Tubs of half-frozen bait stood under the heat lamps, sleet falling steadily outside. Yellow lights.

"I'm glad I'm not going out with you guys on this one," I said, looking at the weather. I half meant it but half wished that I were going. The wind was raw, but it smelled like spring.

"Yeah . . ." Bobby shrugged.

Trying to keep up with them, I fell into the rhythm of something I learned to do long ago from Everett. Chopping bait, each herring in three pieces, swept into the tub. The pieces, not so small they fall off the hook, not so large they were a waste. And gray cod was worth not much more than the herring.

After a time, Gus came back. We moved across the harbor to the crane dock. I kept hacking half-frozen herring into chunks. That first spring fishing must have been on my mind. In the bait shed, I told the story of hitching from Fairbanks and walking the docks in Homer looking for work on a gray cod boat.

"Was it a good boat?" Bobby asked.

"No," I said. "It was the kind of boat you end up on if you don't know shit."

"You can learn a lot on those kind of boats," he said.

"I did," I said.

Then there was silence again, except for the thumping of our knives and the rattle of strangers' voices on the radio. I still didn't like to talk about the years after that first summer. It still hurt.

Nate and I stayed married for eight years. We bought a gill-netter together, the *Tommyknocker*, and fished the Copper River Flats. But our marriage grew worse and worse, whatever love we'd once had eroded by the pressure of our expectations of each other. In the beginning, we had worked together, but as the years passed, Nate grew ever more possessive and controlling, while I became impossible to please. He was driven, I think, by the fear that I did not love him, and I chafed at marriage, as if caught in a trap. In the terrible logic of need, the more he clung, the more I pulled away, until both our hearts were nearly broken.

He wanted me to stay at home and wait for him while he went fishing. I couldn't do it. In the end, we split, driven to it, a terrible but necessary tearing apart. He'd married again within months. But those years were bad enough; I hadn't dated since. I didn't yet have the courage. Even now, I had to remind myself that the love was once real, even if it changed us as it had.

In that short time, though, the world had changed. It was no longer so uncommon to see a woman working on deck. The young men on the *Frisian Lady* never bullied me the way Damon and Travis, and even Nate sometimes, once did. I went back to crewing, and three years later I bought a gill-netter of my own.

The *Solitaire* was a small, old boat, already half-derelict when I bought her. I fished her alone on the Flats. I didn't know enough; I couldn't make it pay, and in the end I had to let her go. But that had been the happiest time of my life, the freedom and the belonging that I'd sought there at last, because the *Solitaire* was my own to love and lose, my own to fish and learn on, too.

Now I was back cutting bait while the sleet fell on the roof, still dreaming of some farther shore, some wider ocean. We pushed the last tubs under the heat lamp. The *Frisian Lady* would leave before morning. I climbed the dock and walked home, thinking of the years to come. I didn't know what was in store. But for now it was enough, this place, this way of being. It was enough we were all still here.